WEED, INC.

WEED, INC.

*The **Truth** About **THC**, the **Pot Lobby**, and
the **Commercial Marijuana Industry***

———————— **Ben Cort** ————————

Health Communications, Inc.
Deerfield Beach, Florida

www.hcibooks.com

Library of Congress Cataloging-in-Publication Data
is available through the Library of Congress

ISBN-13: 978-07573-1988-4 (Paperback)
ISBN-10: 07573-1988-2 (Paperback)
ISBN-13: 978-07573-1989-1 (ePub)
ISBN-10: 07573-1989-0 (ePub)

Publisher: Health Communications, Inc.
           3201 S.W. 15th Street
           Deerfield Beach, FL 33442–8190

Cover design by Jim Pollard
Interior design and formatting by Lawna Patterson Oldfield

Christy, you inspire all that I do. I would have accomplished nothing without you by my side, all that I am proud of in life we have done together. The journey that we are on has been miraculous, even in the mundane, and I owe you everything. Thank you for always being there and for giving me the push I needed to write this. I know it wasn't easy on you for me to invest all of this time writing, but you gave it with grace and understanding that is typical of you.

We did this together, thank you. I love you.

Contents

Acknowledgments xi

Foreword xiii

Introduction:
Who I Am and What I Do and Do Not Care About 1

CHAPTER 1

Decriminalization Versus Commercialization
Have We Been Played? 13

CHAPTER 2

The Evolution of a Plant
God Didn't Make This Stuff 23

CHAPTER 3

The Lobby
Where the Gold's At! 33

CHAPTER 4

Social Justice
That's What This Is All About, Man! 51

CHAPTER 5

Concentrates

710 Is the New 420   65

CHAPTER 6

Vaping

Get High Like a Ninja!   85

CHAPTER 7

Edibles

Brownies? That's so 1970s!   91

CHAPTER 8

Weed and the Environment

There Is Nothing "Green" About This Stuff   109

CHAPTER 9

Law Enforcement

What's Johnny Law Saying?   119

CHAPTER 10

Medical Marijuana

Way *More Complex Than Either Side Is Telling You*   129

CHAPTER 11

In a Perfect World

*Proposed Laws and Their Insanity
Versus Rational Changes*   147

CHAPTER 12

The Arguments and the Rebuttals

*How to Respond to What the
Seventeen-Year-Olds Throw at You*   173

CHAPTER 13

Addiction and Recovery
Yeah, They Are Real Things 197

Afterword:
It's Time We Started Really Paying Attention to
This Weed "Experiment" in Colorado 231

Resources 237

Glossary 241

About the Author 249

Acknowledgments

Kevin Sabet, Monte Stiles, Patrick Kennedy, Chris Thurstone, MD, Laura Martin, MD, David Smith, MD, Jag Khalsa, MS, PhD, Deni Carise, PhD, Evelin Lim Esq, Steve Millette, Mike Cox, Jay Voigt, Adam Pisoni, Sara Urfer, Stacey Harris, Josh Mahan, Jeremy Holburn, John Elliott, Ben Battaglia, Jeff Rasor, Courtney Strong, The Steel Group, Tom Gorman, Kevin Wong, LaTisha Bader, PhD, Chief John Jackson, Chief Marco Vasquez, Josh McClellan, Will Jones, Elyse M, Keith Bradley, Howard Samuels, PhD, Bob DuPont, MD, Tyler Richardson, Rourke Weaver, Bob Ferguson, Gary Forrest, Doug Edwards, Duke, Andy, and NMI.

My mom and dad. I was a pain and you were good to me. I love you both and am doing my best today to help people in the situations I put you in years ago. Thanks for all of your help with this, Dad. I couldn't have done it without you.

Crumb Cake, Rooster, Jelly Boo, you are why I do what I do.

Foreword

In 2016, Ben Cort delivered a powerful presentation at the fourth annual David E. Smith Symposium, the theme of which was marijuana. Ben raised important, frequently overlooked concerns about the risks of making marijuana and cannabis products more available to the public.

In the election that fall, more states legalized marijuana for both medicinal and recreational purposes. With momentum increasing for decriminalization and legalization, commercialization and industrialization of cannabis are not far behind. *Weed, Inc.* examines the many implications of that phenomenon.

Ben informs us, "What the generations before us smoked isn't what kids today are using. The 2 percent THC weed of the Woodstock era is gone; it has been replaced by something with a potency unimaginable a few years ago and consumable in forms that we never thought possible." Those consumable forms include concentrated extracts packaged as candy.

Limited research data suggests that these stronger products may cause more adverse reactions to cannabis use in the short term. As Ben notes, "For the first time ever, cannabis withdrawal was included in the latest edition of the *Diagnostic and Statistical Manual of Mental Disorders* (DSM-5)." No one knows what the long-term effects might be.

When I founded the Haight Ashbury Free Medical Clinic during the Summer of Love in 1967, I witnessed the tragic consequences of the popular idea that drugs were harmless. Voices like Ben's can help us avoid repeating that history.

—David E. Smith, MD

Introduction

Who I Am and What I Do and Do Not Care About

Let's get one thing straight right off the bat, before we even begin this thing: I am not concerned with casual adult marijuana use. So long as kids don't see you (and if they do, realize that it reduces their perception of risk, making them more likely to use before their brains are developed and causing them much more harm), and you are not driving (I don't think I need to make much of a case against driving under the influence), I seriously don't care if an adult chooses to consume weed. As a recovering drug addict, not only do I not get to throw stones, I have no interest in the conversation. We will get into all of this later, but by the age of twenty-five to twenty-six a person's brain is pretty well developed. The likelihood of doing harm to yourself or others because of your use is significantly reduced, unless you're doing something dumb or irresponsible while intoxicated—so just don't do dumb things!

With that said there is potential for harm with any mood-altering substance that intoxicates. I'm not advocating for the adults reading this book to put it down, settle into a comfy sofa, press play on *The Wizard of Oz* and *The Dark Side of the Moon* at the same time while blazing one. If you choose to, however, don't drive and don't let kids see you and I won't say a word against it.

We're only a few sentences in, but I'll bet I've managed to piss off some of you already. The old school of drug abuse prevention is likely unable to reconcile how someone who is so publicly opposed to marijuana commercialization could say something as heretical as what I just did. I can hear it now, "Can you believe this? Now the author is advocating that people get high! He even suggests they do it while watching Judy Garland, God rest her soul!"

At the same time the pro-legalization crowd is likely yelling at the page, "There aren't chemicals in a plant! Driving high isn't nearly as bad as other things we could be doing, not to mention that kids shouldn't be lied to about adult use," or, "It's the same old reefer madness crap. The war on drugs is a failure so back off and stop crusading!"

Warning: If the first few sentences did, indeed, frustrate you, it may be time to put this book down, walk away, hold onto the position that you had when you picked the book up, and keep on keeping on, no hard feelings.

Still with me? Good, because I wasn't writing this for the hard-liners anyway. I'm not putting this together for those so entrenched in the dogma of their own "side" that they will reject anything that confronts the construct through which they view this issue. I'm writing for those of you who are genuinely interested in learning about this complex topic. People who are scratching their heads trying to sift through the news reports to decide what is best for themselves, their families, their states, and their countries. It is for people wrestling with this issue, and for those willing to consider that they may have more to learn. That the experiences on which you have formed your opinion of what is going on with weed and the changing legal landscape today might not be all encompassing. It's tough not to rely solely on our experiences to form our opinions. As Nelson Mandela said, "Where you stand depends on where you sit."

With that last thought in mind it's pretty important that you understand where I sit and how that has influenced where I stand. I have opinions about this that have been formed over many years, and more will come out about what has influenced me, but to start off here are a few highlights. I'm a recovering drug addict and alcoholic, sober since June 15, 1996. I am a resident of Colorado living in Boulder County and working in Denver. I am married and my wife and I are raising three school-aged kids. When I wrote this, I was working for a nonprofit drug and alcohol treatment program at the University of Colorado Hospital and have been in this field since 2007. I am also pretty involved in this issue of marijuana policy both locally and nationally. I'll expand on all of this shortly but I think the bottom line is that I am right smack in the middle of the action and I'm keeping my eyes open. Much has changed in my home state the last few years and, among other things, I hope to give you a street-level view of those changes.

To counter the list of who I am, I now offer who I am not: a doctor. In fact, I barely graduated from high school and earned my first college credits last year at thirty-six. With that said, I can read and understand the scientific process well enough to understand the studies that will be cited. My knowledge on this subject does not come through formal classroom education although I attend *lots* of sessions on the subject at medical and therapeutic conferences. Heck, I even led many of them. Trust me, the irony of a guy like me leading sessions for politicians, doctors, law enforcement, etc., is not lost on either me or my lovely wife!

More often than not, I will shake my head and laugh to myself before taking the stage, stepping in front of a camera, or sitting down with people who truly shape the world in which we live. In my mind's eye I'm still that kid who got sober and learned to live again. I have been blessed beyond belief. I would much rather be working directly with those struggling to overcome addiction, hanging out with my amazing family, or chasing trout with my fly rod than having this conversation. I do so because there is a real need to write this book; I wish there was not.

Alas, if toothpicks were ocean liners we would cross the seas on toothpicks, my wishing isn't helping much. This is a complex subject and I've been avoiding writing this for too long. In what follows I intend to be honest, I hope to be educational, and I trust what I write will be considered.

I care deeply for my home state. My family moved to Boulder, Colorado when I was four years old and remained here until I was twelve when we moved to Northern Virginia, the suburbs of Washington, DC. Home to the University of Colorado, Boulder is a college town with a laid-back vibe; a layover for wanderers with their lives on their backs, most good natured, some intimidating. It's close to Denver but a world away. The foothills of the Rockies are right at the edge of town and you can easily spend the afternoon hiking and fishing. For a kid, it was a magical place to grow up.

Colorado was home to me, even after we moved away, and I dreamed about the day I could go back there to live again. Much of my childhood, my parents were on public assistance and we couldn't afford to return to the Centennial state after we moved away. Still, every so often, I would be reminded of home. I'd see a jay in camp and its call would remind me of the Rockies. The scent of pine trees would make me think of hiking the trails at Chautauqua Park in the shadow of the Flatirons. I'd hear a song or think of a forgotten friend from those years and immediately I'd be transported back to the Colorado of my childhood. We'd camp and climb and fish not only because they were the only forms of recreation our family could afford, but also because we loved to explore. The meat in the freezer was harvested with pride by my father and eventually by us both. The name John Elway was—and still is—to be spoken with awe and reverence at all times. Colorado has always been a paradise on earth in my mind. A place where one can climb ice in the morning up Clear Creek Canyon, climb rock in the afternoon on the Golden Cliffs, and still make it into town for fresh sushi and a show. The opportunity to find adventure in our wilderness and culture in our urban areas is a rare thing. With the robust economy and the opportunities for adventure, one can not only earn a living here but have a good life.[1]

After marrying much further out of my league than anyone should, I returned to Colorado with my wife, Christy, in the fall of 2003. Money was really tight and we needed to have a yard sale in order to rent a moving truck. We had few dollars in our pockets when we got there and even fewer plans that involved much more than a tent, a fly rod, and a climbing rack.

But as I said, I've been blessed. I'd left what I thought to be a promising job in Pennsylvania as a chimney sweep two years earlier for what turned out to be an amazing profession: recruiting. Although

---

1 If this book sells more than the twenty copies that my family and friends will buy, I expect some kind of remuneration from the Colorado Department of Tourism for that last part.

I had no job when we moved to Colorado, this was something I'd started doing before I left the East Coast, and I was able to continue it when I moved to the West. I worked for hospitals and helped them find and hire doctors. It was easy work, paid the bills, and, most importantly, didn't get in the way of our exploration of the state. We took road trips, backpacked, camped, and biked all over the state in the ensuing years. As I reacquainted myself with the land and people, and tried to understand both as an adult, I was able to introduce my wife to this place and it to her. Both were richer for it.

In addition to recruiting, on the side I was a climbing instructor. My father was a climber and I have always climbed. I love to teach, especially kids. For those of you not familiar with the climbing community, it has a bit of a reputation: play hard, party harder. Being the sober guy—I had seven years of sobriety at this point—I was used to being one of a very few who didn't drink or use; it was no big deal to me and certainly no big deal to those I climbed with. One of the few other sober climbers I knew ended up working for me at a climbing gym and we hit it off. We started to climb pretty seriously together. He was a strong ice climber and I had never tried the sport that my father walked away from as too risky. I learned to climb ice and loved it. There are still few things in this world that I would consider more peaceful than the rhythmic ascent of a frozen waterfall far from civilization. It is lonely, demands focus, and can push one as far as they are willing to be pushed. It was on one of these climbs, somewhere in the snow-blanketed Rocky Mountain National Park, that my climbing partner, Scott, and I started kicking around the idea of getting other sober people together to climb. He had a cabin back East in North Conway, New Hampshire, and had thrown a few sober New Year's climbing bashes there. It sounded cool. As we tossed around more about what it could look like, our shared excitement grew. Eventually, he found some money and I quit my job and we started a little non-profit called Phoenix Multisport (PM).

We were careful but also took risks with the business. Keeping the end goal always in mind, *to provide a safe community for those living sober lives to connect with other active, like-minded people*, we watched in awe as PM blew up. Within two years we had a fulltime staff of around ten and were running twenty-plus free events every week. It was amazing. The events, to which we supplied the gear and instruction, ranged from biking, running, triathlon, adventure racing, camping, strength training, hiking, and of course lots of climbing. Before we knew it, thousands of people up and down the Front Range were coming to the events to meet people who expected more out of life in their sobriety than they had found in their years of use. The success got us noticed and we both ended up front and center on the national scene discussing sobriety. Scott actually went on to be named a 2012 top 10 CNN Hero[2] pretty cool!

Hopefully this gives you an idea of where I was coming from when I joined this conversation. Skipping ahead to 2012, we had thirty-ish employees at PM and were running over fifty events every week out of locations in Boulder, Denver, and Colorado Springs. By this time, Christy and I had started a family. The pace needed to sustain and grow PM was frenetic, and certainly not conducive to being an engaged and involved parent. Because of this, I started to consider the appropriate time for me to leave PM. I knew it was the right decision but painful, nonetheless, because I couldn't imagine doing anything other than what I was doing. The rewards, all but monetary, were

---

2 An annual award that highlights the missions of ordinary individuals who are impacting society in incredible ways.

unparalleled and I had never loved work so much. I woke up every day energized and motivated.

I had gotten to know people around the state working at PM and was fortunate to call many with similar passions friends. When one of those friends suggested that I should get involved in politics I was almost as offended as I was amused. I never put much trust in government and less in people who would say anything it took to get a vote. I was also acutely aware that even if I had an interest, people who go through an active addiction don't have the squeaky clean (or at least whitewashed) past that politicians do. We tend to wear our mistakes on our sleeves, and only by addressing them head-on can we ever hope to overcome them.

When my friend went on to explain that it was my experience that would make me good as a person fighting Amendment 64 (A64)—the constitutional amendment authorizing the use and regulation of marijuana/THC in the State of Colorado—I really did laugh out loud. I grew up watching Cheech and Chong and listening to Cypress Hill. I had also smoked a lot of weed, and I thought it was silly that we locked addicts up for possession. We needed more good treatment and prevention in the world and less incarceration. I've always considered minimum sentencing laws silly. Growing up in a peer group where I was one of the few white people, I had seen firsthand the harm that racially disproportionate sentencing could do. I believe I was like most of my generation in thinking that it was no big deal, and maybe even for the best, when I heard about A64.

When I was involved with PM, we had seen a commercial market spring up in 2009 for medical marijuana that was ridiculous—it was often laughable who was using it "medicinally"—but I was so involved with PM that I had paid it little mind. So I told my friend that it really didn't interest me and that I didn't want anything to do with politics. Before parting ways she encouraged me to read over the proposed language on A64 and I agreed.

The law has always fascinated me. I've always liked to review contracts myself before sending them out to council. Something about the binding power of words draws me in. When I did sit down to read over the 3,666 words that made up A64, and that were ultimately to be enshrined within our state constitution, I was shocked.

I expected it to be written from the "live and let live" mentality, a countercultural thumb in the eye of an industrialized prison complex, or a well-considered approach to implementation. Instead, I read page after page spelling out the rights of The Industry and the creation of safeguards for it. Remember, this was an industry that really didn't exist. Not only would it be created overnight, it would be given the keys to the kingdom! Even to a layman like me, the loopholes were big enough to drive trucks through, and after my first read-through I knew I was looking at the christening of a commercial industry. *This wasn't about freedom. It was, and is, about big business.*

That was it for me. I knew for sure I needed to leave PM, not only because of my family but because I now had a new mission. My last day was on our annual trip to Moab in May 2012. Around a campfire with 120 recovering addicts and alcoholics, I said my farewells and they said theirs to me. It was bittersweet, and I still miss those days. But I made the right decision; I knew I had to act.

I'll discuss my time with the A64 campaign in more detail later, and at that point you will likely see why the largest tattoo I have is a big "politics be damned" image. Following the election of 2012, when we passed A64 in Colorado, I decided that I was done with all things addiction and got back into recruiting. I made it three months before I knew I needed to get back to working with those on the front line fighting addiction. I took a job with the University of Colorado Hospital in their substance-use disorder treatment program, CeDAR (Center for Education Dependency and Addiction Recovery) and was a proud member of that life-changing team until January 2017, when I left to focus fulltime on consulting and educating about THC. In the pages that follow, I will heavily draw upon my experience over the last several years working at the tip of the spear battling addiction.

One last note about my experience. Two days after the election that enshrined commercialized THC into our state constitution, I got a call from a guy I liked and had gotten to know a bit throughout the campaign, Kevin Sabet—or Dr. Sabet, if we're making dinner reservations. Kevin came out to Colorado once or twice to talk politics with the campaign and we hit it off. While we are almost exactly the same age, our paths were as different as they could be. Kevin grew up in Orange County, California, and went on to Berkeley where he made noise as a student senator and advocate for drug prevention and human rights. At that time, I was mastering the art of gravity bong construction and committing grand theft auto. Following Berkeley, Kevin went on to Cambridge where he studied public policy as a Marshall Scholar, writing his doctoral dissertation on drug policy. While he was being appointed to his first of three White House staffs, I was watching addiction kill friends and was starting to allow myself to dream of what sobriety might look like.

So Kevin called me a couple of days after the vote and told me that he was thinking about starting an organization that would promote the scientific aspect of marijuana use in public policy. He felt like the scientific and medical communities were too absent from the conversation and had some cool ideas to get them more involved. We kicked the idea around a while and I got excited. I loved the notion of helping to create a platform where the opinions of those who mattered most would be heard. Shortly thereafter, Kevin called again to tell me that both President George W. Bush's speechwriter David Frum and Democratic icon Patrick Kennedy had reached out to him and were deeply concerned and wanted to do something to help. Kevin told them about the organization, and Smart Approaches to Marijuana (SAM) was born.

In the months that followed, SAM came into the national spotlight. We all spent a lot of time talking to the media and discussing the importance of incorporating sound science into drug policy. Kevin has become a dear friend and encouraged me to stay involved in this conversation.

Kevin and Patrick went on to recruit a world-class board of directors, composed of doctors and scientists, to help inform our positions. SAM would emerge as a global thought leader in the marijuana conversation. I remain on the board of directors, made up of some of the finest minds in the world on this subject. They keep me around for the street view, for the recovery perspective, and probably because they feel sorry for me. I'm the only one on the board without an "alphabet soup" after my name! Much that I have learned in the years since has come from these sources.

I will spend the following chapters elaborating on that politically charged statement: "This wasn't about freedom, it was about big business." In addition to my own experience from the street view in Colorado, I have access to some of the finest minds in the nation on this subject and will present their opinions and findings, even when they do not align with mine. As I hope to illustrate, this conversation is too important to allow dogma or preconceived ideas to dictate the future. We owe it to ourselves and to future generations to consider this issue from all sides.

One more note before we get started: I had to make some decisions about the size of this book project, and while it may seem long, it's not comprehensive. This issue is changing daily and what follows isn't exhaustive, but it's a good starting point aimed at educating and encouraging conversation. There isn't one book that could sum up everything about weed, so take what follows for what it is: an overview and a conversation starter. I've had a hard time not trying to sneak in more every single day since this book has been "done," but I've added what was determined to be the most relevant and I had to streamline much of that. As the old quote goes, "If I'd had more time, I would have written a shorter letter," I have tried to keep this thing concise.

I'll apologize in advance for my prose. I am an avid reader and while I have never quit on a book (*Zen and the Art of Motorcycle Maintenance* almost got me; six months to wade through that one), I have always been critical of what I perceived to be poor literature. I more or less write this in the same tone that I speak. I hope it isn't distracting and that you can see past my inexperienced hand to the truths I intend to present.

CHAPTER 1

Decriminalization Versus Commercialization

Have We Been Played?

The first thing I think we need to establish is the language. You may have noticed already that I shy away from calling what happened in Colorado "legalization." Whether or not that word is accurate, it doesn't fit the reality of what happened, nor does it fit the meaning that most people assign to it. To the majority of the world, "legalization" is essentially decriminalization. We hear it said and imagine a place where people are no longer locked up for having a dime-bag in their pocket, where an adult doesn't fear law enforcement kicking in the door when they are smoking a joint in their basement. Honestly, I have never seen anything wrong with a society like that. Casual users of illicit substances shouldn't be locked up, in my opinion, and in reality they seldom are, although we are told a very different story. The realities of incarceration around marijuana need more space than a few sentences in this chapter, so I will spend more time on it later.

What I have come to learn, along with many other Coloradans, is that what most thought was simple decriminalization was really commercialization. And that it goes far beyond a plant that can be found in nature and was used for thousands of years by ancient societies. The law was written to not only support but to create a commercialized market for THC. Every "recreational" law passed since (Washington, Oregon, Alaska, Massachusetts, California, Nevada, and Maine) has followed suit.

I realize that I may be getting ahead of some readers' understanding already when I say "THC." We need an effective working definition of this thing that I will refer to a good deal moving forward. THC, or tetrahydrocannabinol, is the chemical responsible for most of marijuana's psychological effects; in other words, the part of the cannabis plant that gets you high. Without THC, cannabis is basically hemp, and the more THC there is in the plant the higher one gets consuming it. THC has few, if any, medicinal qualities, and according to a recent study[3] published in the prestigious journal *The Lancet*, more THC equals more psychosis and mental illness. It's also important to note that THC can be consumed in many different ways; it can be smoked, eaten, vaporized, and absorbed topically. While there are a few examples recently of people snorting and injecting THC, neither is a very effective method of ingestion so we won't be covering those at all. In A64 marijuana is defined as:

---

3 Feb 2015 Volume 2, No. 3 p. 233–238

MARIJUANA OR "MARIHUANA" MEANS ALL PARTS OF THE PLANT OF THE GENUS CANNABIS WHETHER GROWING OR NOT, THE SEEDS THEREOF, THE RESIN EXTRACTED FROM ANY PART OF THE PLANT, AND EVERY COMPOUND, MANUFACTURE, SALT, DERIVATIVE, MIXTURE, OR PREPARATION OF THE PLANT, ITS SEEDS, OR ITS RESIN, INCLUDING MARIHUANA CONCENTRATE.

What's "marihuana concentrate" you ask? *Much* more on that later. The point is that we did not just protect the plant, we protected the right to manufacture and sell every imaginable byproduct, derivative, and component that can be made from the plant. Think of it like not just sugar but everything you can make with sugar. The guys who penned A64 didn't make a mistake with this definition; they knew exactly what they were doing. Both are lawyers who had dedicated their careers to marijuana law and these guys are experts in the field. While the majority of people, even people in my industry, didn't have any idea what a concentrate was and thought that edibles were just baked goods that left your teeth full of stems, Brian Vincente and Christian Sederberg knew better. In addition to being experts on weed, they are shrewd lawyers who recognize the legal difference between a "should," a "may," and a "shall." Their role and rise to stardom will be discussed in a later chapter, so back to the vernacular. "Commercialized" works better than "legalized" and "THC" is more accurate than "marijuana."

To say that we simply "legalized" the plant is misleading and brings us to the first major point where I ask you to step away from the preconceptions you have about marijuana. This is about commercialized

THC and The Industry that supplies it, in all its forms, to the public. As of this writing, the City and County of Denver has eighty-plus more retail marijuana stores than McDonald's and Starbucks *combined*. While these weed stores do sell a form of the actual cannabis plant, much of the commerce done is in concentrates, edibles, and THC that can be vaporized. In a few short years we Coloradans have become world-renowned leaders on the extraction of highly potent THC from the plant, and its manufacture into an almost unimaginable amount of ways to consume that THC. The intersection of a mind-altering substance with American-style capitalism is a reality in Colorado, and one that has had predictably ugly results.

To support the crowded weed industry that has sprung up and that continues to grow at breakneck pace, two things must happen:

1. Current users must be converted to more frequent users.
2. New users must be created and captured.

We can't have the number of stores that we have in Colorado and expect them all just to fight over existing demand; that's just Econ 101. When supply outpaces demand, demand must be created.

None of this would be a problem if we were talking about something totally harmless, say, the sale of roses. If tomorrow we suddenly became the rose capital of the world, producing roses of a higher quality at a greater rate than anyone else would be no big deal. Sure, there would be unforeseen consequences, we might run out of land to grow roses and might have issues with water needed and the infrastructure to ship them out, but for the most part it would be pretty benign. Unleashing a hoard of rose merchants in Colorado driven by a need to sell more roses to keep their doors open would do nothing more sinister than making Colorado smell nice. The fact that they would be driven to sell us more and more roses to support their business wouldn't matter much. The principle is the same: to support the growing commercialized industry, Colorado's THC salesmen need to sell more weed to stay in business. This business is unlike any other that I can think of in that The Industry has no federal oversight, and it has grown at a pace that's made building and enforcing responsible regulation totally impossible. It is also a product with such amazing potential for refinement that allowing that refinement without proper oversight has led to pandemonium on the ground—and it's just getting started.

I'll give several examples to support the statements above. One of the easiest to get your brain around is soda. Ten years ago, the idea of drinking THC would have gotten a good laugh in most dispensaries. It wasn't one of the ways that we got high and for lots of reasons would have been something that I think most people would have frowned upon. Following the commercialization of THC in Colorado, I started to notice a diversity in "edibles" (candies, cookies, chocolate bars, that kind of thing) that was alarming. The first time I saw an ad for THC-infused soda I was floored. Soda? Sugary, carbonated, easy-to-conceal soda! Per Colorado's law limiting THC in edibles and infused products, the first THC soda I saw had the legal limit of THC, 10 mgs. A few months ago, I came across an ad for a soda with 350 mgs in the bottle. Keef Cola offers flavors including Cherry Bomb, Blue Dream, Lemon Lime, Purple Passion, etc., and they have managed to get 350 mgs of THC in each bottle, along with plenty of sugar. Under Colorado law that means that each of those sugary, carbonated, pop-top bottles has thirty-five individual servings in it. Here is a perfect example of an industry racing to innovate and making a product that is insanely strong with no regard for how safe it may or may not be.

Now for the regulation side. All we have to do is tell them to knock it off, right? Get these guys to put a more responsible dose in their soda, stop with the cartoon characters being used to sell it—you'll see plenty examples of that in this book—and make them package it in a way that makes consuming thirty-five legal servings all at once hard. What we hear from The Lobby spokesmen is that they want this to work worse than the naysayers, that they are the ones with their livelihoods on the line, so of course they will be responsible! We could say that with great power comes great responsibility. The Industry will regulate itself because no parasite kills its host; they don't want us to turn against them before we all have a chance to see how easy this all was and how well it will work worldwide. If you take those kinds of statements at face value, I have a bridge I'd like to sell you.

We don't think about much in this country past this financial quarter's return. If we were *really* forward thinking, we'd focus on next quarter. Cash rules everything around me (props to those of you who finished that verse in your head) and *the job of business in America is to make money.* If a soda with 350 mgs of THC will make money then, in a way, it's the job of The Industry to sell that soda and get paid!

In Colorado, state committees have been meeting to establish regulations about how to mandate packaging indicating that what's inside can get you high—really, *really* high in many cases—but so far all of the proposals have been struck down or sessions have ended in gridlock. Many manufacturers came out strongly opposed to any regulations. They were afraid of the cost and the trouble it would make for them to implement these regs. At the forefront of the pushback was Dixie Elixirs, the biggest manufacture of THC soda in the world. The company argued that dividing bottles into individual serving sizes would cost a fortune, and labeling each serving as containing THC would mean spending even more. Their CEO made over $900,000 last year and has $26,000 in stock options. I'm okay with their margins slimming down a bit in the interest of public safety, but apparently *they* aren't! The owner of Dixie Elixirs, a guy named Tripp Keber, said in a speech in 2015 at BevNet, an alcoholic beverage industry conference in New York City reported in *Inc.* magazine, "I fundamentally believe that it is Big Alcohol and Big Tobacco that will be my future employer."[4] *Sound like the weed industry you were expecting?*

To make sure that the message about packaging got across to the politicians, a few more lobbyists were added to the payroll and more contributions were made to political campaigns. After a few more palms were greased in the political game, sure enough, the committee punted on the issue and a few more financial quarters were secured to sell whatever Dixie Elixirs wanted, however Dixie Elixirs wanted.

Forgive me for complicating an act as seemingly simple as selling soda, but there is one more aspect to consider: federal oversight.

Each summer, when my daughter and the next-door neighbor set up their juice stand, I'm pretty sure they are breaking about a dozen federal laws and a few state laws. I keep thinking about asking them to have their customers sign waivers but I'm not sure if that would implicate them further should they ever fall under the gavel; parenting is so confusing. There is a valid reason for rules and regulations as administered by the Food and Drug Administration (FDA), the federal agency tasked with food safety. This includes the manufacturing process, the people who work in The Industry, and

---

4 *https://www.inc.com/will-yakowicz/dixie-elixirs-thc-infused-edibles-denver.html*

the impact of producing the products on the environment. Companies that are negligent, and put people at risk, can face criminal charges and also negligence lawsuits brought by consumers. While sometimes I do think we live in an overly litigious society, I'm glad these people are out there making sure we aren't eating things that are going to hurt us.

When it comes to marijuana and its safety for consumers, however, the FDA has no oversight authority. Why? It's because marijuana is an illegal substance at the federal level, and it doesn't look like it will be changing anytime soon. Since it's illegal, the FDA would be complicit in breaking a federal law if it played a role in oversight of products made with THC. So it's hands-off for the FDA when it comes to Keef Cola and Dixie Elixirs. The massive infrastructure, well-funded checks and balances, and standard operating procedure doesn't matter when it comes to the commercial pot industry. The state has to build its own function to match the feds, but their budget is miniscule by comparison and they are in a fierce battle with companies flush with cash from selling the edible products the agencies will be charged with regulating. Kind of wild, right? You would think we would have given this some consideration before passing the laws. There is a chapter coming up about how this really came about that will explain how words become laws. I promise it's going to piss you off.

So, back to our use of language, *decriminalizing* something makes it so that users and possessors don't get arrested. *Commercializing* makes it okay to manufacture and sell that substance to the public. We have commercialized THC here in Colorado. With this more accurate definition in place, think back to the news stories you may have heard coming out of Colorado; they have been about the industrialization of THC far more than they have been about decriminalizing marijuana. CNN ran a series called *High Profits*. The "Green Rush" is commonly used to describe the money being made. Recently I read a story entitled "How You Can Cash in on Legal Marijuana." This is about The Industry selling the THC, not about the end user consuming it. The final chapter of this book discusses my vision for how we can go about refining drug laws to have more common sense, and proposes solutions to problems that have long faced our society. Spoiler alert: those solutions look more like decrim and much less like the laws being put forth by The Lobby that are being voted on all over our country.

CHAPTER 2

The Evolution of a Plant

God Didn't Make This Stuff

God made weed. George Washington, the father of our country, grew and probably smoked it. The Chinese have been using it for millennia to treat a variety of conditions. Cannabis grows naturally and that's a good thing. I love having conversations with people who point out these facts because they are true. Finding things to agree on with the pro-weed crowd is refreshing, even if it does little to advance their position that THC should be commercialized. We can agree that Genesis 1:12 says, "And the earth brought forth grass, the herb that yields seeds according to its kind . . ." That our first president did most likely grow, and at times, smoke "hemp." Marijuana is listed as one of the fifty fundamental herbs of traditional Chinese medicine (TCM). We can agree on those things. We agree that the fibers of the plant were a valuable cash crop giving us textiles galore—and hanging rope—back when our founding fathers did their thing and needed that stuff.

We can also agree that it was a plant/drug that was demonized, and much of that demonization clearly had origins inside the deep-rooted and institutionalized racism that defined many of our laws in the eighteenth, nineteenth, and early twentieth centuries. The way "the man" hated and persecuted weed undoubtedly had much to do with the hatred and desire to persecute people of color and other immigrants in this country.

What the pro-weed lobby has done masterfully is take up these centuries-old uses and decades-past injustices to peddle their THC. They have convinced much of this country that to hate racism and embrace old-timey ways is to consume genetically modified, mass produced, pesticide-ridden, energy-hungry weed being sold by corporate interests and private equity money. The alternative we are presented with is sold as social justice when, in fact, it is just another money grab; capitalism rather than altruism.

In this chapter we will take a closer look at how this plant has evolved and what the reality is today.

If I read the closed eyes and unenthusiastic faces correctly in the audiences to which I often present on this subject, the historical significance of hemp isn't what people are interested in hearing about. They want to know how this changing landscape affects their lives today, and how 40-plus percent THC, potent weed changes things. In many ways what was going on around marijuana even five years ago is antiquated information. We want *current* information. To understand that current information one needs a little bit of history, so bear with me!

We first need to realize that while there are hundreds of chemicals found inside the cannabis plant, two are by far the most interesting:

THC and CBD. *THC is what gets a person high; CBD is another type of cannabinoid naturally occurring in the marijuana plant, and is where we find the most interesting potential medicinal benefits.* While we can't be sure exactly what is naturally occurring inside the plant (it's been selectively bred for too long to increase the high) we do know that the natural levels of THC and CBD are under 1 percent. We also know that, in one of nature's little miracles, CBD counteracts the psychedelic effects of THC. In other words, if the quantities of CBD and THC are equal you will have a hell of a hard time getting high by smoking/ingesting the plant. So *nature gave us a plant with potential medicinal benefits that have very subtle intoxicating effects.*

For fifty years we have been collecting samples of marijuana from all over the country and analyzing them in a lab at the University of Mississippi. What we have learned as shown in the graph below is that we have become better botanists over the years.

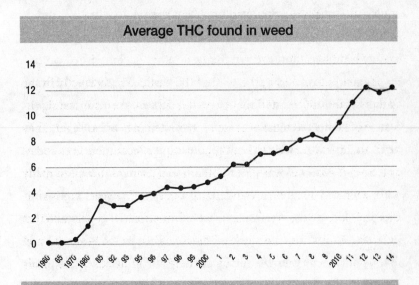

Average THC found in weed

We have learned how to breed marijuana into what we want: a drug that gets us higher. As CBD has stayed the same, under 1 percent, THC content has risen to average over 12 percent nationwide back in 2014 resulting in a much more potent drug. In Colorado, a 12 percent sample would be very hard to find, we are seeing plants pushing past 40 percent today.

When I stopped getting high in the summer of 1996, the national average of THC found inside marijuana was under 5 percent. Back then we got our weed out of Southeast DC, and it was arguably some of the best on earth. Our stuff came into the nation's capital through direct channels and was sold to us by kids, grandmothers, and serious gangbangers on 203rd Street right after coming in from Galveston and off the wharf. Our bud was world class. It was also likely around or under 10 percent THC.

I remember smoking once with a dedicated stoner in rural North Carolina; let's call him "B." B got high daily and assured us that he could out-smoke anyone we knew back home and that we didn't know anything about weed because we weren't smoking good ol' Smoky Mountain homegrown. Being a rather accomplished cannabis consumer myself, I warned B that DC weed was as wicked a thing as there was out there and that he would do well to take it easy. I was assured that his tolerance was super high from his daily use and that he could take what we had without breaking a sweat. Thirty minutes and one joint later, B was passed out on the ground unable to say his name while we giggled and rolled up another. We ended up leaving that poor kid on his own in a field, no doubt wondering what train hit him. It was the chronic train straight *outta* DC! By today's standards that would hardly even be "ditch" weed. It sure as heck wouldn't pass for anything here in Colorado where we regularly see weed advertised as containing over 30 percent THC and where much of that weed is "infused," meaning it's sprayed with concentrated THC and then sold. The percentage of THC that stuff contains is anybody's guess.

Let's let that sink in for a minute. Thirty-plus percent THC is the norm now in Colorado, post-industrialization, and often that is just the starting point!

Recently, we have seen a few very credible studies that tell us why we should be concerned with higher potency weed. It turns out that more THC is likely very bad for one's brain. While we have yet to study anything stronger than 16 percent weed officially, what we have learned from the studies is that the higher the THC the higher the likelihood of psychosis and the lower the function of the corpus callosum, a part of the brain that consists of nerve fibers responsible for communicating between the two halves of the brain. *More THC not only reduces the brain function of very healthy areas, it likely promotes dysfunction in areas that lead to severe mental illness.* While The Lobby scrambles to cover these studies up and question the sound science behind them, our kids keep getting the message that weed is a natural and safe substance that should be used to promote good mental and physical health. While these claims can be easily refuted scientifically, the message that weed is safe and natural has had its desired effect; more and more kids are getting high and the business owners are raking in the money with no thought to the long-term effects of what they are promoting.

Ten years ago, the idea of 20 percent THC in weed was a pipe dream. If somebody said they had something that potent, the editors at *High Times* would have laughed them out of the room and asked for some of what they were smoking. We didn't think that much THC could be crammed into marijuana. This lack of foresight didn't take into account a virtually unregulated commercial market and the power that money has to drive innovation. We therefore didn't start any long-term studies on the effects of real-world weed, so the science is *way* behind The Industry.

The reason why studies need to be longitudinal (long term) lies in the very nature of marijuana as a drug. It is not something that devastates the user right away; it's a slow burn, so to speak. Weed takes a while to have negative effects on users, it doesn't typically happen overnight. This is one of the reasons why marijuana addiction is so hard to treat. By the time people recognize they have a problem and seek help for it, they have typically been going down that road for many years.

To better illustrate what I mean, if you were to put down this book and start smoking meth a few times a week we would see the negative effects on your life pretty quickly. You would become physically dependent on the drug and would likely do all kinds of stuff that would be huge warning signs to those who loved you. They would know pretty quickly that you were on a pathway to destruction and would pull out all the stops to get you help.

On the other hand, were you to put this book down and decide to make THC a regular part of your life, it wouldn't be as noticeable to your friends and family right away. They might laugh about it with you and talk behind your back about subtle changes they noticed, but for the most part you wouldn't have them calling an interventionist to get you into treatment right away. We might check back in a year or two later to find that you still had a job, didn't have multiple driving-under-the-influence charges, and were doing okay. We might also find that you had moved back in with your parents and gotten *really* good at "Call of Duty" (that's a popular video game, old people). In my field, we don't typically see someone who has had the wheels come completely off within a short time of starting to smoke weed. While this isn't the case with other forms of THC, for example, concentrates, it makes early intervention much harder and therefore treatment more difficult. It also drives home the importance of long-term studies.

To understand the negative effect that THC is having on a person's life, it takes time, sometimes several years. Furthermore, studies looking at the effects of THC take time to produce. That doesn't mean we can't make some pretty solid guesses about what we will see with a higher potency weed, but we can't say empirically. As potency has increased so has the need for credible long-term studies on its effect but rather than wait for the results our federal government has decided to allow The Industry to drive the market and make super-high-potency weed the norm. Unfortunately, that genie can't be put back into the bottle. Crazy strong weed is here to stay. To me, that means that we had better start to change the narrative around marijuana in this country.

As I write this, a Colorado-based nonprofit group called "Smart Colorado," has begun a billboard campaign aimed at changing the dialogue. Their mission is to: "protect the public health and safety," especially for Colorado youth as marijuana becomes commercialized and increasingly available. The billboards are simple but profound. Over the face of a child covered in the Colorado state flag it asks the question, "Dad, is today's pot a hard drug?"

Not only do we need to ask this question, we need to demand that our politicians answer it, especially those enjoying huge campaign contributions from The Industry. *What the generations before us smoked isn't what kids today are using.* The 2 percent THC weed of the Woodstock era is gone; it has been replaced by something with a

Dad, is today's Pot a hard drug? Learn about potency SMARTCOLORADO.ORG

potency unimaginable a few years ago and consumable in forms that we never thought possible. Passing a joint while listening to Joe Walsh is a different experience than popping a handful of gummy bears, each containing ten times the legal limit of THC per serving, and then hitting a 90 percent THC dab on a super-heated needle because the high hasn't kicked in from the candy yet. Eating a brownie baked with weed inside isn't the same as drinking a sugary soda with 350 milligrams of THC flavored like sour apples and clearly packaged to be consumed in one sitting. *We have little idea what those more potent forms of THC are doing to the brains and bodies of their users, but The Industry doesn't seem to care as long as there's a dollar to be made.*

Let's get back to the question, "Is today's pot a hard drug?" Any "no" argument to this question will have to find roots in the historical use of marijuana, not in the reality of today. Today's pot is not what your grandfather smoked, it's not what your father consumed, heck it isn't even what I smoked! It has been specifically bred, modified, and manufactured to pack the strongest punch it can possibly hold. *This is not an argument about marijuana or cannabis, it's about THC.* The sooner we realize this, the sooner we can start making laws that reflect the true nature of today's situation. What we are dealing with today is an industry promoted by a lobby hell-bent on getting people to ingest

THC any way they can. If that means they put it into a cookie then so be it. "Repurposed" candies? You bet. Concentrates? Even better.

You might be surprised by this list of THC-infused products:

Coffee	Breath spray
Ice cream	Intimate oils
Frosting	Pills
Baked goods	Toffee
Suckers	Granola
Cotton candy	Caramels
Soda	Gum
Tea	Marinara sauce
Hot cocoa	Baklava
Breath mints	. . . and the list grows every day.

People today are not just smoking weed, they are popping it between classes, sucking on it while driving, drinking it before work, chewing on it while talking to you, and eating it as dessert. *THC is not only stronger than ever before, it's increasingly in everything you could ever desire and we are gobbling it up with no thought to the consequences.* We can't just talk about weed, we need to understand and talk about THC and the consequences of ingesting this kind of THC in these new kinds of ways. There is nothing counter-culture about consuming THC, nothing historically relevant, nothing promoting healing. Today's THC is mass produced to be as strong as possible and mass marketed to get into the bodies of as many people as possible. When today's consumers hear "weed" they are thinking about THC in all its ever-evolving forms, not a plant found in nature—are you?

CHAPTER 3

The Lobby

Where the Gold's At!

The Weed Lobby. What do those three words make you think of? Stop for a moment and let the mental image come into focus . . .

If you're like me, you are picturing some aged hippie in a tie-dye shirt, Birkenstocks, fanny pack on, crooked, wild eyebrows and long white hair in a ponytail, holding a clipboard asking you to sign a petition to "unchain the herb." We think of the old burn-outs at NORML (the National Organization for the Reform of Marijuana Laws) smoking doobies and complaining about cops and politicians; it's actually a pretty fun crowd if you ask me. I could sit for hours with these guys talking about Led Zeppelin and biodiesel, sustainable farming and global warming, civil unrest and tolerance—good stuff! Because people like this are true believers, they are interesting.

While we might not agree on everything, I have a hard time looking down on someone who believes passionately in something, even if that something is different than my beliefs; it's that kind of relationship that makes life interesting.

The kinds of people who make life incredibly uninteresting, predictable, and frustrating are the carpetbaggers: the people who follow money as the *only* truth and who will do *anything* to get paid. This is the THC lobby in America today. Hippies and NORML have been replaced by Troy Dayton at Arcview, F. Aaron Smith at the Cannabis Industry Association, Ethan Nadelmann at the Drug Policy Alliance (DPA), Mason Tvert at the Marijuana Policy Project (MPP), Brendan Kennedy at Privateer Holdings, Justin Hartfield at Weedmaps by SAFER, The Marijuana Industry Group, The International Cannabis Association, The Marijuana Trade Association, and the Marijuana Growers Association of America. And of course Brian Vicente and Christian Sederberg, two of the architects of A64 whose law firm was named one of "the most powerful people" in Denver by *5280* magazine in 2014, and whose website proudly states, "Building The Industry" at the top of their homepage, to name a few.

These guys don't wear tie dye and carry clipboards. They are lobbyists and privileged white guys (seriously, they are all white and rich) in $5,000 suits carrying smartphones and being followed by personal assistants. They drive Mercedes not Subarus and have more money at their disposal than you and I will ever see in our lives, all stored up for one reason: *to get you to consume, and keep consuming, THC.* The more THC you consume the more they make, the more lawyers they can hire, and the more politicians and voters they can influence. The more laws they change the richer they get. Like most things in this country, it's all about the money, and people are literally lining up in

Colorado to give them theirs. The first day of recreational weed sales, customer lines stretched around the block at shops all over the state.

When the battle over A64 was raging in Colorado, I was surprised by the constant vitriol. The first threat of violence that came in over our website freaked me out when I saw it and I was surprised to see my coworkers, political veterans, laugh it off and tell me that it was commonplace in this campaign and that I shouldn't worry at all about it. I had an idea of what civil discourse was all about and figured that the debates and arguments would be informed and interesting. I wasn't expecting bomb threats and people telling me they hoped my kids got hit by a bus at events. My ignorance was quickly replaced by the wisdom that comes with experience, and I came to expect that kind of "passion" from the other side. Initially, I was also surprised by the seemingly endless resources that the pro-64 side displayed compared to the lack of money raised by our campaign. I had no idea how the deep the pockets of the pro side were—and still are. With that said, one of the most surprising things I saw in the campaign's first few weeks was when I actually came face to face with our opposition. We were doing an event—at the Denver Press Club, as I recall—and it came to our attention that we would have protestors present. I expected a group of guys in T-shirts carrying cardboard signs. Instead, I saw Mason Tvert of the Marijuana Policy Project in a *very* nice suit, leading a small group of people dressed equally as well, passing out flyers with counterpoints to many of our arguments. The sheets were professionally produced—full color and glossy—full of half-truths and misrepresentations of the science. I was shocked. This initial experience with The Lobby left me scratching my head. How did these guys get their money? What drove them to show up with their crew *everywhere* we were to cast doubt on objective science and get as much media time as they could? The explanation was a well-oiled machine that had been built and paid for by the DPA and the MPP, two groups I had never heard of before the campaign to commercialize THC in Colorado. Since then, I've learned of the depth of these organizations and others, and the drive they have to influence policy so that they can get paid.

If the legalization movement had a family tree, the rich uncle would be the DPA, and its godfather would be George Soros, the billionaire investor, business magnate, and philanthropist. The DPA is a policy group out of New York City run by a PhD/JD named Ethan Nadelmann. He first came on the scene when he was appointed to the board of directors for NORML in 1984. With the financial backing of his longtime friend George Soros, Ethan went on to found the Lind-smith Center in 1994, a group that would eventually rebrand as the DPA in 2000. With the help and funding of Soros, as well as others who sit on their insanely well-funded board—like Richard Branson, Sting, Harry Belafonte and of course Arianna Huffington (co-founder and former editor-in-chief of the Huffington Post)—the DPA claims to be the brain and war chest behind California's first in the nation "medical" marijuana laws, in addition to all of the "recreational" laws that have passed in the last few years. Their huge staff boasts seven full-time employees in their "office of legal affairs." The org chart at the DPA would make the nonprofits I have been a part of green with jealousy at the obvious resources it takes to run such an organization. In fact, they are so well funded they have their own grant-making division working to "promote policy change and advance drug policy reform at the local, state, and national levels." These guys are policy experts working to change laws over time to be more friendly to users and dealers.

George Soros

In addition to their professional bench, the DPA also has an unrivaled network of volunteers that can be called on at a moment's notice to protest or advocate as directed. Thousands upon thousands of people, mostly young people, are on standby, ready to advocate for the DPA's positions.

While Ethan is the front man for the DPA, there is no question about whose resources underwrite much of the expenses. George Soros is by far their largest contributor, donating in excess of $100 million. As one of the thirty richest people in the world Soros is a controversial figure. A notorious "short seller," the mention of his name makes my conservative friends go pale and cross themselves. In 2005, a French court convicted Soros of insider trading.

As a philanthropist he has given away billions over the years to various causes but it would appear that the apple of his eye is the DPA and their work to change drug laws. Since Soros has made his billions speculating on the market it doesn't take a rocket scientist to guess his intentions. In a recent TED Talk, Ethan described the global drug trade as a "commodity market" that isn't being taken advantage of. I can guess who would like to control some of those "commodities."

In an issue of *The Economist* (July 26, 2001) Nadelmann is quoted as saying:

"The best answer is to move slowly but firmly to dismantle the edifice of enforcement. Start with the possession and sale of cannabis and amphetamines, and experiment with different strategies. Move on to hard drugs, sold through licensed outlets."

Make no mistake about it, this debate is about unleashing the "global commodity market" that is drugs—all drugs. Fortunately for us we have vast experience on this subject in America, we need look no further than alcohol and tobacco. These two legal drugs give us a good idea of how "regulated" sales work in our style of capitalism. Let's ask ourselves, did we nail it with alcohol and tobacco? Is our country a better place because we have these substances so readily available and advertised? I don't know about you, but if I could go back in time a hundred years and fight like hell to keep big tobacco from becoming what it is today I would do it in a second. I would do whatever it took to get our nation to think a few years down the road instead of just react to what the budding industry was feeding us.

In Colorado, we know of no less than twenty-eight full-time lobbyists dedicated to protecting and advancing the financial interests of the THC industry. To date, there are no dedicated lobbyists working to oppose their interests, and why should there be? There's no money in it! Ask yourself, Joe Public, "How do you expect to get honest and unbiased facts about this issue when so many people are working so hard to advance only one side?" I realize this question cuts to the very heart of politics and the money behind it, but I can't avoid the discussion. I want us to look to the specifics of this issue. **We are considering a massive shift in policy that will result in more access to a substance we know little about in its current form. We must not allow the conversation to be defined just by those who stand to profit.**

I often hear the undefined "they" referred to when discussing how these laws come into being. I believe that most Americans think laws are crafted by benevolent politicians pulling all-nighters with their staffers, weighing the best evidence, the pros and cons of each sentence to make sure that what is put to a vote is in the best interests of those it will affect. We believe that knowledgeable and thoughtful leaders dedicate huge amounts of consideration to what will become law in this country. The reality is that most politicians are too busy eating good steak and drinking good whisky to be bothered with actually crafting bills. They are provided with "sample legislation" that is given to them by those buying the steak and whisky. Lobbies write bills, politicians present and vote on them. The weed legislation being considered and voted upon is crafted by rich Uncle DPA. *Concerned much less with the harms of their sample bills than they are with increasing the profit margin of the commodity market, these bills are not about anything other than making money.*

A dear friend of mine works with troubled youth in Denver. I won't say more because I can't compromise the trust in which this story was relayed. He had been working with a young man for several years who was finally terming out of their program. Prior to intervention, this youth's future was bleak. He has a functional IQ of 72, meaning that he was just above the minimum threshold below which he would be given permanent disability by the State of Colorado for life. Since the State deemed him just capable enough to navigate the world on his own, he would have to work. My friend helped him get a part-time job in the fast food industry and find a roommate. His life wouldn't be the kind of thing books are written about, but it would be okay.

On the day he was being discharged from his recovery program, the employees of my friend's underfunded service agency threw a party with their own money celebrating the young man's success and wishing him well as he set off into the world on his own. While eating cake and sharing a few laughs, my buddy noticed the young man on his phone. He stepped closer to listen, and could hear the young man make arrangements for his friend to buy him an ounce of weed. Exasperated, my buddy quickly confronted him, reminding the youth that weed wasn't going to help him and that they had all fought hard to get him to his substance-free state. My friend, with tears in his eyes, recounted to me the young man's response: "Dude, if it was bad for me they wouldn't have legalized it." Think about that. This young man had such confidence in the "they" making this decision that he was going to celebrate by getting high. By consuming a substance that that leads to up to an eight-point IQ loss in those who use it regularly[5], the same as lead poisoning. He believed that the State was looking out for him; it wasn't. A constitutional amendment written by the THC lobby had won out, convincing him that his life would be better spent high. He was assured that the consequences were nothing to worry about because "it's just weed." In the end, some dispensary would pocket another $100.

I believe that it is our responsibility to look out for the most

5 Proceedings of the National Academy of Science of the United States of America vol. 109 no. 40 Madeline H. Meier, E2657–E2664, doi: 10.1073/pnas.1206820109

vulnerable in our society, those who have the deck stacked against them, the disenfranchised, the less fortunate. Are we willing to let their futures be defined by The Lobby, which sees them as nothing more than willing consumers of their commodities?

My friend Will Jones did something absolutely insane a few years ago. He stood up to the weed lobby in Washington, DC. As a young African-American man in our nation's capital he was supposed to be in a demographic that was locked up, and one that would vote with the DPA legislation. Will didn't see it that way. He saw the harm that drugs, and specifically marijuana, had done in his neighborhood and decided to push back on the legislation being pushed on him. Will started a true grassroots organization and went about fighting. He debated, wrote and performed rap songs, and slam poetry to get the word out to his peers. He was relentless in his opposition to a bill that would eventually pass and open the doors to the THC lobby in DC. In my mind, this is what America is all about: one man willing to fight back, and to stand up for his community in the face of insurmountable odds. Rather than winning praise for his efforts and given consideration for his position, The Lobby demonized Will and eventually sued him. They so hated his dissent that they did all they could to destroy him. With the help of some pro bono work from a local lawyer, Will eventually got his life back but not before he learned an important lesson: if you fight The Lobby, be prepared to face the consequences.

Sadly, I will know that this book has found its mark when I am further set upon by The Lobby. It is astonishing to me the amount of energy that gets spent trying to silence any opposition to their efforts. I recently went to Michigan to give a few talks. I was warned by one of the groups that there was chatter on social media that was threatening enough that they suggested I keep a pretty low profile and ride to and from events with police when possible. As someone with nothing at all to prove, I gladly accepted my rides (got some cool pics of Dad with the police for my six-year-old) and went about giving the talks. On my second day, I was greeted by protestors at the venue with signs and chants. They were willing to stand outside in a Michigan winter to protest the presence of someone who dared raise another perspective. They then proceeded to follow me around the state protesting the events. I knew I was on the right path.

Last year, I went to Texas Christian University (TCU) to participate in an event for the student body about weed. It was a debate-style format, which I don't like because there's usually too much emphasis on soundbites over science, but I love talking to young people. I was also invited to meet up with the TCU Students for Recovery Peer Support Group on campus while there, so I jumped on a plane. I was to be opposite a gentleman named "Radical" Russ Belville. An outspoken proponent of marijuana, Russ airs a twenty-four hour legalization talk show *The Marijuana Agenda with Russ Belville* 420radio.org.

In addition to being up to date on the most recent science and trends, I prepare for debates by very deliberately humanizing the person I will be sharing the stage with. As a person in recovery, it's super important to me that I never make any of it personal and that I don't get angry when debating. I want to make sure that I get the chance to shake hands with my opponent and to get to know him or her a bit. I don't think people are "bad" or "good"; we're all just people doing the best we can with what we have, and I like to spend some time with the other side to remind myself of that fact.

When I arrived on campus in my little economy rental car (scary as crap when navigating Dallas during rush hour) I noticed the Marijuana Policy Project (MPP) SUV parked out front. It was wrapped and covered with weed plants and their logo. I smiled to myself and walked in. Russ was accompanied by several young men who did their best to make me feel uncomfortable by surrounding me and standing inside my personal space.

I introduced myself to them all, shaking hands and making small talk. I asked Russ to step aside for a moment, and I thanked him for making the trip. I told him a little about myself and tried to steer our conversation away from weed; nobody wants to be one-dimensional, and I wanted to know the man, not the debater.

We went on to have an interesting debate that was frustrating at times because I felt like people were less interested in the data and more interested in "zingers." But in the end I left feeling positive and grateful to have been asked to have that important conversation with students. I was a bit surprised when Russ brought up my own recovery in a negative way a few times, but such is life. What really caught me off guard was hearing what he had posted on Facebook around the debate. I don't do anything on social media, I hardly have time to keep up with the friends in my life as is! So when a buddy showed me the posts it was all news to me. Prior to the debate he posted:

> "I almost feel sorry for the guy, Ben Cort. Then I remember that he supports testing my piss to determine my character, using cops to enforce sobriety, and incarceration of minorities at disproportionate rates. So f—k him. He gets my complete and undivided attention tonight, when I'm through he will wish he was still smoking pot."

While there is nothing wrong with getting amped up for the debate, I'm not sure what the "testing my piss" thing was all about and some of the other claims made me chuckle. It wasn't the same spirit that I had hoped for in our debate but . . . whatever.

The post following our event was when it got good:

> "I just would not let Ben breathe without bringing it back to punishing adults who choose marijuana over beer (thanks Mason Tvert) and that this is about marijuana markets that have and will always exist (thanks Peter J Christ) and that what we're really talking about is freedom, not marijuana (thanks Keith Stroup)."

It was interesting to me that he came back to "marijuana markets" and the tagline developed by MPP superstar Mason Tvert. It is also important to note that his conversation, and that of other proponents, is most often about freedom rather than marijuana. By making it all about freedom we ask people to disregard the specifics of the conversation and associate it with something that we love in America—and especially in Texas.

He goes on in the same post:

> "Ben only had his commercialization scare . . . He tried to evoke sympathy for the poor marijuana addicts like him who suffer the smell of marijuana all around Denver; I stiffed that with 'as a guy recovering from obesity, I hate smelling that doughnut shop by my house'. . ."

While I remember much of the debate differently than Russ, I do recall the exchange around the smell of weed in Denver well. My first reaction to him saying he was a food addict was compassion. Eating disorders are a huge and growing problem in our society and I have plenty of friends who have struggled with them; they are actually more lethal in many cases than chemical addiction. We see lots of eating disorders with our patients, it is very serious business. My sympathy disappeared pretty quickly when I realized that he was making fun of the daily fight I and many others have to stay sober and was taking a shot at people who really do struggle with food-related addictions. The point I had made was that nobody cares about responsible adults who want to get high, but The Lobby feels like it is their right to allow for open consumption, and the smell that accompanies it, to be anywhere in Colorado and the rest of us just need to adjust. I resent the fact that my kids now know what weed smells like because it is everywhere in Colorado and that it doesn't make things easier for people like me to constantly be smelling it wherever we go.

Let me say again that I don't care if you smoke weed, but it's not your right to make *me* smell *your* weed for the same reason I don't have to smell someone's cigarette smoke. In this regard, it is very different from alcohol. I don't walk down the street on a summer night in Boulder and smell beer in the air at every corner. The idea that I was being mocked for saying I didn't want to smell weed everywhere was pretty surprising, but the biggest takeaway from those posts was the total disregard for any opinion other than the one he came in with.

If evidence presented during a debate proved an opponent's position was correct, I wouldn't hold fast to my position at all costs. The day I do that is the day I stop taking the stage. We should always be willing to change our minds for the better; dogma be damned. When

I debate about weed, I often feel like I am arguing with people who are so entrenched in their belief systems that challenging them threatens their fundamental self-perceptions. Further complicating the issue is one's livelihood. When a person's paycheck and belief system are woven together, he or she becomes territorial, because a change in position would mean a loss of income. They are stuck defending a job instead of contributing to a rational conversation. A paid lobby exemplifies the worst of this argument.

So, back to The Lobby issue. I just stepped away from writing to grab some dinner. While waiting to order my burrito I picked up the newest edition of *Boulder Weekly,* a free local independent newspaper that always has interesting articles you won't find in the commercial dailies. While thumbing through articles about renaming Columbus Day to "Indigenous Peoples Day" and getting mountain bikes to the women in Boulder's sister city in Afghanistan, I came across something interesting opposite a full-page ad for pre-rolled packs of joints: "The Gummy Bear Dilemma." This article discussed pending legislation in Colorado that would require THC candy makers to indicate that their candy contained THC. The fact that this is even up for debate proves my point about the power of The Lobby. The article said, "(marking candy as containing THC) is a substantial hiccup in the business operations for marijuana-infused product companies and one that comes at a considerable cost." The journalist goes on to quote Nancy Whiteman, spokeswoman for the Cannabis Industry Alliance (CBA), "The CBA, and I think The Industry at large, were very supportive of the child-resistant packaging regulations because we can clearly see how that helped public safety and helped keep it away from children. But the CBA is under the impression that the previous rounds of labeling and child-resistant packaging sufficiently dealt with the potential for accidental ingestion. What we have been asking for, as an industry group, is please show us the data that there is in fact even a need for this."

Okay, let's recap: the generous people at the CBA claimed to love the idea of child-resistant packaging. (Truth be told, The Industry fought tooth-and-nail, claiming undue regulations like this would hamper their profits.) The CBA really doesn't see an issue with gummy bears that contain 100 milligrams of THC, ten times the legal serving size, being totally indistinguishable from regular gummy bears. They first want data showing that regulations that aren't in effect anywhere on God's green earth will be helpful before they agree to stamp their THC candy so that parents don't accidentally give it to their three-year-old. Seriously, have we lost our damn minds?

Sounds a lot to me like the argument that candy cigarettes aren't bad because they are clearly candy. But candy cigarettes can't lead to death or hospitalization—unlike THC-infused candy. Hospital admissions for children under twelve who accidently consume THC are up 800 percent.[6] So, again, unless we've completely lost our minds, why is this even an issue? It's because the weed lobby and The Industry it supports puts its profit margins ahead of the well-being of our kids. Heaven forbid that they have to endure a "hiccup" in their ability to buy gummy bears in bulk, lay them on a table, spray them with a concentrated THC, repackage and sell them. These poor lost souls might have to forego the upgraded rims on their brand-new Escalade if we lay all of this "crazy unnecessary" regulation on them. As it stands right now, one of the most reliable ways to tell if a gummy bear in my home state contains THC is whether or not it has been

---

6 Rocky Mountain High Intensity Drug Trafficking Area. *The Legalization of Marijuana in Colorado: The Impact,* Volume 3, September 2015, p. 77.

rolled in sugar. Many of the weed-gummies get a healthy coating of sugar added to them before resale—but not all. Bottom line, you better read the packaging pretty carefully before you rip open that bag and let your kids dive in.

In other news, Colorado legislators considered a bill that would make manufacturers declare that their weed is pesticide-free but it was DOA. After the recall of literally hundreds of thousands of pieces of candy and marijuana plants, we are taking another look at how to make sure that harmful and illegal pesticides stay out of the weed people are smoking and eating. In October 4, 2015, *The Denver Post* published a story, "Deep Dive: Why Colorado Has Struggled to Regulate Pot Pesticides" about the issue. Because commercial weed is grown indoors, in large concentration and in close proximity, the plants are vulnerable to mites and mildew that can rapidly destroy the crop. Growers were thus using very hard-hitting and potentially dangerous pesticides to keep these things in check. The Industry pushed back on regulations and the federal government, which regulates pesticides, didn't provide guidance because marijuana is not legal federally. The *Post* article recapped three years of e-mails and records it had obtained about the regulatory resistance. It said: "State regulators struggled with the issue while the cannabis industry protested that proposed limits on pesticides would leave their crops vulnerable. . . . Last year the state was preparing a list of allowable substances that would have restricted pesticides on marijuana to the least toxic chemicals, Colorado Department of Agriculture stopped the process under pressure from The Industry, *The Post* found." John Salazar, the former Agriculture Commissioner is then quoted as saying, "The marijuana industry was the biggest obstacle we had." Starting to believe me about the deep, dark lobby yet?

Mark candy as having THC? Keep known, harmful chemicals from being ingested by the public? Hell no, not if it gets in the way of their bottom line.

An article by Associated Press reporter Kristen Wyatt entitled "Biz Owners Replace Idealists in Pro-Pot Movement" shows how much the philosophical tide has shifted in the push for marijuana legalization laws, from one of personal freedom to one of big profit centers. It begins with the following:

"Business owners are replacing idealists in the marijuana legalization movement as the nascent cannabis industry creates a broad base of new donors, many of them entrepreneurs willing to spend to change drug policy . . . They constitute a bigger coalition of business interests. And their support provides a significant financial advantage for the pro-legalization campaigns."

So tell me, who is pressuring our politicians from making simple commonsense changes to keep our state a safe place to raise kids? Is it Grandpa and a clipboard, or the marijuana industry and their lawyers? I'm pretty sure Grandpa isn't donating millions of dollars to their reelection campaigns.

CHAPTER 4

Social Justice

That's What This Is All About, Man!

Maybe you've heard this argument for legal weed: "Social justice. That's what this is about, man." Not exactly. I live just north of the city of Boulder. In addition to being affectionately referred to as "The People's Republic of Boulder" for its left-leaning political views, Boulder is also a strong contender for the NIMBY capital of the world: **Not in My Back Yard!**

Working in addiction treatment, I know a thing or two about the whole NIMBY scene. Everybody wants more places to treat addicts; nobody wants them near where they work, live, or send their kids to school. People are able to keep programs out of their neighborhoods if they have the means to fight them. They are successful if they can turn out at community meetings, hire attorneys to fight for them, organize petition drives, and convince key opinion leaders to side with them. It takes large amounts of time and lots of disposable income to make those things happen, two things that are in short supply in poor and minority communities.

The same NIMBY principle applies to weed shops. A very visual indication of this can be found on the website www.weedmaps.com. Justin Hartfield created this little beauty to make it easier for us all to find weed for sale (he also refers to himself as the Phillip Morris of weed but that's neither here nor there). If you know Colorado at all, and specifically Denver, one of the first things that should jump out at you, as you try to wade through the 700-plus shops in Colorado on Weedmaps, is where they are all located. If you're not in front of your computer to cross reference or don't know the area, I'll give you a hint: NIMBY!

In an effort to give my kids a very different experience than I had growing up and to provide them with a different caliber of education than I received, we choose to live in an upper-middle class suburb that is about as diverse as Connecticut; in other words, it's filled with white people. Boulder isn't the most diverse place to begin with—it's maybe the whitest place on Earth outside of Norway—and my community is no exception. Notably, we don't have a single dispensary near us; the closest is about eight miles away in the middle of the intersection of 66th Street and US 287. It's new and is somewhat remarkable because the purple-and-yellow paint scheme once prompted my six-year-old to ask me if it was a toy store.

Anyway, we don't have dispensaries here because nobody wants a dispensary in their neighborhood and we have kept them out. When I say "nobody" I mean nobody—not just white nobodies. Fortunately, where I live we have the necessary ingredients for a dispensary-free neighborhood: time and money. Mix those two together and the

Green Tree Medicinals, Longmont, Colorado

parents will win out every time; they won't be able to set up shop here anytime soon.

Now that you understand where I live, I'd like you to understand where I worked while writing this manuscript. Because I was so in love with my job and the people I worked with and believe that I worked in one of the most amazing treatment centers in the country, I drove forty-two miles each way to get to and from my job. To the conspiracy theorists who think my position on this issue is influenced by my need to get people into rehab, know that this is a nonprofit program that doesn't ever accept patients who are mandated to treatment. They are the good guys. I'm talking about the University of Colorado Hospital, one of the top-rated academic medical institutions in the country. The facility recently moved from east Denver to an amazing new campus in a suburb of Denver called Aurora. Located just north of Colfax Avenue on the grounds of the old Fitzsimmons

Army Medical Center, it's not necessarily in the safest part of the metro area.

I left my house around 8:00 most mornings to drop the kids off at school and then jump on the Denver-Boulder Turnpike to begin my journey east. At 8:15 I pass almost close enough to my first weed shop to smell it. There are two pretty close to one another, The Farm and The Green Room. These two shops are up north and a bit out of place. My guess is that they are there because there isn't much residential around other than a few trailer parks (we have three in Boulder) so nobody cared much. The real shopping district for weed in Boulder is on The Hill, right off of the CU campus, check www.weedmaps.com.

Moving on, I don't pass another dispensary for a long time (although I am traveling on highways that have been "adopted" by weed shops/manufacturers and noted as such), until about 8:55, when I exit I-225 onto Peoria Street and turn south. It's at this point that I know to roll up the windows and hit the little recycled air button in my truck because the smell of fresh weed still does something to this addict's brain. Towering above the takeout, check cashing stores, pawn shops, and gas stations are two huge warehouses where they grow and, of course, sell weed.

Across the street there is a big sign directing motorists to another warehouse/store. Within a quarter mile of exiting, I pass four shops. As Dorothy would say, "Toto, I've got a feeling we're not in Kansas anymore." Things really get interesting if I forget to turn into work (heaven forbid) and go down to Colfax Avenue, the most infamous street in Colorado—if you watch *South Park*, you've likely heard about it—because of the preponderance of vice-squad activities, and hang a right. I'll start seeing the pot shops immediately, one of which has a big flashing sign out front to make sure I know where to get my

THC Medical and Recreational warehouse in Aurora

weed. Continue driving five minutes or so and I will hit the "Green Mile" a section of Colfax so concentrated with weed shops that I could stand in the middle of the road and hit four with a rock without moving my feet.

If I had turned left onto Colfax, I would have passed Panera, Chipotle, coffee shops and a Smashburger, but no weed shops. These businesses are the kind of places that pop up when a neighborhood gets gentrified, and have emerged to support the new medical center. But if we continue our journey westward, we immediately start passing pawn shops, a few hair-braiding salons, tobacco shops, and the first weed business, The Green Garden Center, directly adjacent to Jumbo Discount Liquor. Things start to get really thick once you pass Monaco Parkway. You know what else is thick there? Low-income housing and lots of economically depressed neighborhoods that are disproportionately inhabited by minorities.

Bottom line is that weed shops aren't in the nice neighborhoods. They are in communities where people have to fight harder to stay above water. It's this fact that allows me to call BS every time somebody pulls out the social justice card. To say that we are doing minority communities a favor by filling their neighborhoods with more drugs isn't okay. Proponents leave this out when they tell us about how many black people are arrested for drug possession rather than white people. The thing that kills me is that it distracts from the real conversation: why do so many more people of color live in places that are economically disenfranchised? Why do they earn less money? Why are so many more arrested? Why do they get harsher sentences? The reality is that racism is alive and well in this country and continues to hold people back regardless of the fact that we elected a black man to lead our country not once, but twice, and have made a lot of progress in many ways. When we talk about allowing commercialized weed as a way of treating racism, it's like considering a sneeze without looking at the cold. The problem is that we have spent the last few years talking about sneezing and doing nothing to address how sick the patient really is. We aren't talking about the continued presence of institutionalized racism in our judicial system and how pretty much every judge and prosecutor is a rich white guy, we are talking about arrests (more commonly citations) for possessing weed. People seem less concerned with addressing income inequality and educational issues than legalizing another commodity they can get rich off of. Want to know the real kicker? *Pretty much everybody who owns these shops is white.*

I read an article the other day about the huge race divide in the weed industry and how there weren't enough minority owners. The article went on to feature an African-American woman who owns a dispensary. I can't imagine how much effort it took to find her! Keep in mind that banks can't finance weed shops because it's illegal federally. To open one up you have to come into the game with a ton of cash. You need money to buy the building, renovate, purchase supplies, hire employees, and, most importantly, advertise. The people who open those shops don't live in those neighborhoods; they live in places that make mine look like the 'hood. They make money selling drugs into poor and disenfranchised communities and the whole time The Lobby tries to sell us on social justice. It seriously is enough to make you pop off if you think about it. The last thing these neighborhoods need is a drug that reduces school success (the drug suspension rate, almost entirely attributable to weed, is 110 percent higher in schools with the highest population of minorities than those with the lowest[7]), intoxicates and hurts families, makes it harder to get good jobs (people still drug test here), and leads to increased crime. Maybe before we let rich Joe White Guy tell us what we need, we should ask the people trying to raise families in these neighborhoods what they think.

On January 4, 2016, *The Denver Post* finally broke this story in an article entitled, "Denver's Pot Businesses Mostly in Low-Income, Minority Neighborhoods." Reporters interviewed people from the neighborhoods saturated by pot shops; these folks were not happy. In one neighborhood highlighted in the article, there is one weed shop for every forty-seven people, and depending on where you are in that neighborhood it's 70 to 90 percent minorities who live there. I recommend reading the entire article, but if you don't, here is one of my favorite quotes: "You would think that we've borne our fair

---

7 "Marijuana Legalization in Colorado: Early Findings" published by the Colorado Department of Public Safety, March 2016.

share already," said Candi CdeBaca, a member of Cross Community Coalition in Globeville [a Denver neighborhood] and longtime resident there. Her home, in the family since her great grandfather, faces a large marijuana grow. "We've been around, and it happens over and over."

One man interviewed in the article, Drew Dutcher, vice president of United Community Action Network, noted that it is far easier to find a dispensary in his neighborhood than a grocery store—the closest one is almost two miles away. "People here usually shop for groceries at the 7-Eleven," Dutcher said. "Something's out of balance." I agree. When the only green plant you can find to ingest in your neighborhood is weed and not a vegetable, we are seriously out of balance.

Some THC CEOs claim they are for the downtrodden. A little later in the article, one of them talks about how her company has given away veggies to local residents "grown in the company garden." Seriously, that's an exact quote. She is quoted as saying, "It was really cool to sit there and meet the community." Meg Sanders is her name, and she is also quoted as saying, "We are passionate about doing what we can as a tiny little business doing our part in education and awareness . . . and hopefully helping the neighborhood." According to her profile on www.womengrow.com, Ms. Sanders "Heads the largest woman-led cannabis company in America." She owns an infused product manufacturer and medical and recreational dispensaries across the state, and is working on opening stores in Illinois. The profile also says that her company is "engaged in an aggressive growth strategy" and is on track to double production and distribution outlets over the next six months. I wonder how many of those shops will be in *her* neighborhood? Pretty likely that her "tiny little business" will keep growing in places where the people don't look like her or have their kids in private school. The reality is that it's much less likely that Meg and her well-heeled friends consume THC at the same levels as her less-fortunate customers. According to statistics in a March 2016 report by the Colorado Department of Public Safety entitled "Marijuana Legalization in Colorado: Early Findings," regular THC use drops as income levels rise. For instance, 19.8 percent of people with incomes of under $25,000 a year consumed THC in the last month. In the $25,000 to $49,999-per-year income bracket, it drops to 12.3 percent. Finally, of those earning over $50,000 per year, only 11.1 percent report consuming THC in the last month.

For the most part I don't think there is some big conspiracy about getting weed shops into poor black and Hispanic neighborhoods; although there are probably people who are specifically targeting these neighborhoods, just like there are people likely specifically targeting young people by opening up close to schools. Despite the fact that there are regulations prohibiting proximity to schools, they are rarely enforced.

A dispensary two blocks from an elementary school.
That's Cookie Monster with a plate of weed next
to the ice cream and candy.

I doubt that there is a dedicated effort by The Industry to saturate these neighborhoods; it just kind of happens. Not only is there more money to be made in these neighborhoods, the zoning is clearly a bit friendlier with commercial and industrial often in close proximity to residential. Who knows why? Is it because the folks representing these places don't care or don't have the influence to change things? Is it because people who don't live there own lots of the buildings and place their return on investment higher than the quality of life for those in a place they never visit? Is it because that's how America does things, the poor can't fight back as well in our system so their voices don't get heard? Is it a combination of all of these?

I don't know what the answer is but, as Candi said earlier, "It happens over and over." If there is money to be made selling a vice substance most of it will be made in poor neighborhoods, and poor neighborhoods in Denver are mostly minority. If we haven't figured out how to stop this by now I doubt we will with THC. Certainly part of the solution is to have fewer stores that sell vice substances—pretty damn simple. We could also force the weed industry to behave more like the alcohol industry they keep trying to compare themselves to by making community approval of new licenses mandatory. I'd love to see how that would play out! Would the rich white guys who own big weed companies want to live across the street from them? Have their kids go to school next to them? It could be fun to watch that conversation. Unfortunately, that won't happen anytime soon. Money buys political influence and The Industry is awash in money, so it's back to the status quo.

Sorry, Candi, the family home is probably worth more now as a site for a grow house or a "bud-and-breakfast" putting up all of our pot tourists. Maybe you could make enough selling the place to get out of a neighborhood now infested with weed. I'm sorry that nobody listens; apparently Colorado and The Industry know what's better for your community than you do. Clearly, they thought they knew what was better for your kids but unfortunately they were wrong there as well. The first data we see[8] shows that youth arrests for marijuana increased ever so slightly, 2 percent since THC commercialization. However it gets real when you consider that there was an 8 percent reduction in arrests of white kids, a 29 percent increase in arrests of Hispanic youth, and a 58 percent increase in the arrests of black kids for marijuana crimes. You read that right, we are arresting fewer white kids than before and *a lot more* black and Hispanic kids. Does this sound like "social justice" to any of you? Please Carl Hart, justify that nonsense.

One of the foulest examples of this total disregard for minority communities came in the Alaska general election in 2014. The DPA gave a few people some legislation to introduce and then hired a guy, Taylor Bickford from Seattle, to run the campaign to commercialize THC. The first major endorsement for the "No" campaign came from the Northwest Tribal Council, a group representing the interests of Native Americans all over the Pacific Northwest, including Alaska. They were up in arms about a law that would basically undo the gains that had been made by restricting the flow of alcohol in populations with high rates of addiction. The "dry" or "damp" laws, as they are often known, had made it illegal to possess or sell alcohol in certain towns and villages. If the DPA-crafted legislation were to be approved, it would make it impossible to outlaw the possession of THC anywhere in the state, and the Tribal Council was nervous about what

---

8 "Marijuana Legalization in Colorado: Early Findings a Report Pursuant to Senate Bill 13-283", p. 8.

would happen when another intoxicant was introduced and made readily available to their people.

The No campaign was then approached by a really amazing guy named Mike Williams. Mike is a native Alaskan, a United States Army veteran, and has run the Iditarod sled dog race fifteen times. The race covers 1,000 miles and is a grueling test of physical endurance and emotional fortitude. Mike knows all about resilience beyond the race. He lost all of his brothers to alcoholism, but, instead of going down the same path, he has dedicated his life to preventing substance abuse and suicide in youth. When he mushes, he carries pledges from thousands of people committing to sobriety. Needless to say, he has won many accolades and is a local hero. Mike became the head of the No campaign and the primary spokesman opposing commercialized weed.

With their spokesman from Seattle (whose father is now a full-time paid lobbyist for the Alaskan weed industry) and hundreds of thousands of dollars from the DPA in New York City, the proponents of the bill were able to buy a big enough bullhorn to push their agenda, no matter how reckless it might be, especially to the Native Alaskan community, which has suffered disproportionately from the ravages of substance abuse. The DPA was essentially saying: "Silly Indians, we know best, trust us." The history of this country is full of examples of this willful disregard and dishonesty, so I won't take the time to elaborate on the painfulness of the mentality here. Basically, they said that the native people didn't matter, that they would be better off by letting white folks do what they felt like doing so they could get paid. I know that this sounds harsh but what happened *is harsh* and I won't apologize for calling it out. I have worked with Native Americans whose lives and cultures have been wrecked by substance abuse. If you want to see harsh, spend a few days on a reservation, not in a casino.

All this talk of social justice by The Lobby is a smokescreen, a way of distracting us from the real agenda— getting paid. My grandfather used to play this "game" with me when I was a kid. He would stand over me and make a fist then shake it and say, "Watch my hand, watch my hand," then *bang!* Out of nowhere his other hand would get me. It was years before I realized that the waving hand wasn't what I had to worry about.

CHAPTER 5

Concentrates

710 Is the New 420

I recently gave a talk in Colorado Springs at one of my favorite events in the field, The Winter Symposium on Addictive Disorders. It attracts a national audience but its core is people working in the addiction field in Colorado, from all walks of life and backgrounds. This was the forty-second year the event had been held and, as always, was full of fantastic information for those of us in treatment and healthcare. My talk was focused on the changing legal THC scene, locally and nationally. I was asked to address up-to-the-minute changes in the laws. Before getting to that part I gave a quick overview of the science and trends in use. I hadn't intended to get too far into trends since these are people on the front line of treatment in Colorado, and they know this stuff as well as anyone anywhere. When I asked for a show of hands of those who were familiar with concentrates, less than ten hands went up in the room of about 300, so I decided to spend some time talking about them. This form of THC consumption is so new that not even the people in *that* room knew much about it. This was honestly pretty scary.

Before I get started I want you to consider that for the under twenty-five crowd, *concentrates are marijuana*. This is what they think of when someone says "weed." Concentrates are everywhere and are not just being used by the fringe; they are mainstream and they are what many people picture when we talk about marijuana. You are going to think some of this must be talking about hardcore users on the edge, but it's not; concentrates are everywhere and have become synonymous with weed for this generation of users.

It's tough to know where to start when talking concentrates, so I think I'll try to give you a visual first. Concentrates come in a few forms ranging from a thick oil or a buttery substance to a hard, rock-like form; think of a flat Jolly Rancher. Things in this form obviously can't be rolled into a joint and smoked, they aren't malleable like a plant is, and won't combust at temperatures as low as organic substances will. Concentrates need about 700 degrees to combust, so they are best consumed on a superheated needle, a hot knife, or in a vaporizer built to get that hot. I'm guessing that many of you are scratching your heads right now wondering what the hell I'm talking about. That's good! I'm glad that most people don't know what it means to hot-knife a drug! Typically, I'm not a big fan of all the drug porn that Hollywood and the news media throws at us but it will help you here. Think of images you have seen of people smoking crack, meth, and heroin; concentrates are smoked the same way.

Rather than rolling a joint with buds or other parts of a weed plant, a concentrate is broken off from its rock-like form, put on something that is hot as hell and inhaled. Traditional crack pipes actually work very nicely.

Not exactly what you envision when you think "weed," right?

Now that you know what they look like, let's talk about what they do. In a nutshell, they get you stupid wasted, stupid fast. Since concentrates typically contain 80 to 95 percent THC, a little bit goes a long way.

Look at the ad on the following page and see the recommended dosage. Tell me America, when is the last time we did anything "half the size of a pinhead"? In fact, one of the loudest arguments in support of concentrates is that since they are so insanely strong people will consume less of them and it will all be good. We will get into that one later, but let's be honest, it's a total nonsense argument that makes sense to some people at face value but doesn't even begin to pass the giggle test for those of us who know how this stuff works in the real world. When you go to YouTube and watch people using concentrates (search "first dab" for some of my favorites), you will notice that very seldom does somebody take a dab hit alone, at least not until they have built up a tolerance and can. Concentrates hit so hard that those "half the size of a pinhead" puffs very often put experienced weed smokers on their backs within a couple of seconds. You need what's

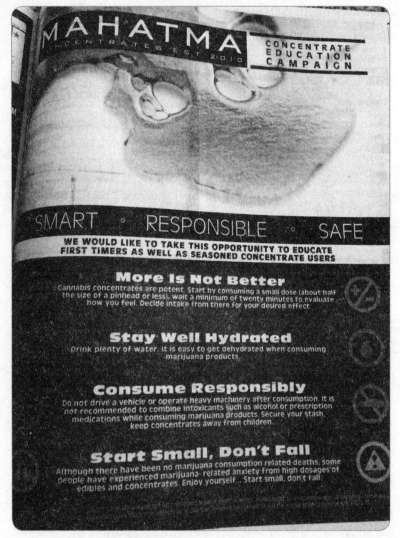

Suggested consumption is "about half the size of a pinhead or less."

called a spotter to be right there so that when you pass out, someone can catch you before you hit the floor, or have the trash can ready for when you vomit the contents of your stomach. Seriously, watch a few videos. There are tens of thousands to choose from; it's wild stuff. If you watch nothing else on YouTube click on this one: "Kill a Friend Day" by StonersRWeed.

What We Know About Concentrates and the Brain and Body

Now that we know what they look like and how to consume them, it's time to learn about what they do to your brain and body. After consulting the finest minds in medicine and addiction treatment, and taken it upon myself to gather every single bit of scientific data we have about what an 80-plus percent THC product does, I've discovered this, summarized below:

- ✓ Um, yeah
- ✓ *Soooooo*, concentrates, right?
- ✓ Well, we think . . . maybe they . . . could be . . . never mind
- ✓ They are scary

There it is, everything that science and medicine knows conclusively about concentrates gathered in one place.

There are, however, a few people doing research on the subject. One is Dr. Christian Hopfer, a brilliant doctor I have the pleasure of working with. Still, because real scientific research is a painstaking process, requiring considerable time for accurate study, peer review, and publication, it will be some time before we know the results. What doesn't take time is an unregulated industry whipped into a frenzy of innovation, driven by easy money to take advantage of new opportunities to get into your wallet. If any other substance was being sold in our country the way this one is, we would have researched and regulated the crap out of it before letting it out for distribution and consumption. Unfortunately, regulators and the public—even those in my field—still think we are dealing with a Model T when it's really a Lamborghini. We're trying to build a regulatory infrastructure to keep the public safe from something that needs a hand crank to start and tops out at 20 miles-per-hour downhill with a tailwind, when in reality these guys are driving 220 miles per hour around town, laughing the whole way. .

Without empirical data, we have to look at anecdotal accounts, so forgive me while I tell you a few stories of what driving 220 miles-per-hour looks like. First, I want to refer back to the aforementioned study published in *The Lancet* in March 2015. This study shows a significant increase in psychosis for individuals who use "high-potency" weed. In that study, high potency was defined as 16 percent THC.

I'm pretty immersed in the treatment and recovery world. I travel a lot, and because of that I have gotten to know many people who work in this field. One of the groups of people who are most consistently misunderstood are the interventionists. If you ever walk into a room and your whole family is sitting around and there is some stranger in the middle holding a bunch of letters, don't freak out; it's a good thing! While sometimes portrayed in films and television shows as jackasses—and some can be bad, as in any profession—very few truly operate like that. They are amazing, compassionate people who love helping addicts and alcoholics and their families enough to jump at the chance of sitting in a situation like that where they are sure to be hated before they even talk.

One of the most amazing interventionists I know is a guy named Keith Bradley. He works for a quarter of what he could charge, and often works for free when people really can't afford it and need the help. He once told me he is working to repay a debt that is so large he doesn't have enough life left to settle it up. I don't know many people who love addicts and alcoholics as much as Keith does. He takes calls around the clock and will jump in the car or on a plane on a moment's notice to help someone suffering. He is almost always successful. I've personally watched him break down walls in minutes that took decades to form. Keith gets people to see the light and want to go to treatment. He says that people are always relieved to be in an intervention because nobody wants to live like that, not really; it just takes them a bit of convincing to realize it, and when they do they are relieved in many ways.

Keith truly is a miracle worker who tears up every time we talk about an intervention, but he won't intervene on concentrate users anymore. "I would rather do an intervention on a heroin addict who has been shooting dope in the street for years than try to intervene on someone who's been using concentrates for six months," Keith told me. After another unsuccessful intervention attempt on a young concentrate user—the only time I've seen him fail—Keith was at a loss. The situation he described was beyond frustrating and broke our hearts. There was nothing he could say or do to get through to this young man; he kept ringing the proverbial doorbell but nobody was home.

After this incident, Keith had a change of heart. He drove to my house recently, notebook in hand, and asked me to tell him everything I knew about concentrates. Keith told me that he had done some serious soul-searching and decided that he was wrong to write off so many addicts; he told me that he was going to learn everything he could about the substance so that he could help, not walk away from people who needed his help. Based on the calls he was getting, it was impossible to see concentrates as "anything less than a pending epidemic" and he needed to be ready.

Some of the most frustrating calls I get at work are the people calling for loved ones who are smoking concentrates, often eight or more times a day. They are seeing the total wreckage that living perpetually über-stoned is creating in their lives, but the users just don't seem to get it. There is a condition often associated with heavy marijuana use called "amotivational syndrome" that likely accounts for some of what we're seeing with concentrates. While there is no solid evidence, I see it all the time.

If you're not yet ready to call for a total ban of concentrates, keep reading. I don't think that concentrates have any place in the world, based alone on what I've told you already. I believe they should be banned totally until we have more evidence on what they are doing to users in the short and long term. If all of that didn't do it for you, maybe this will: concentrates are made by creating little bombs. Those bombs are often made by people often under the influence and in residential areas. What could possibly go wrong?

I suggest taking a few minutes to look into some of those news stories. You'll undoubtedly find them in a quick Internet search. But first, you should first understand the process for making concentrates or "butane hash oil" (BHO). If you would rather not look at one of the 1.1 million sites that come back after a quick Google search, or watch one of the 367,000 videos on YouTube (or the one on the *Denver Post's* site) teaching you how to make it, I will give a quick overview:

It helps to have a *bunch* of "trim." Because we have a massive industry here, trim is pretty much given away. It's the part of the plant that is trimmed off when getting buds ready for sale.

- ✓ Take the trim and cram a bunch of it into a PVC or metal pipe.
- ✓ Force compressed butane in one end of the tube and let the liquid drain out the other.
- ✓ Follow one of any number of routes to "purge" the BHO. Purge is the word they use to describe trying to get as much of the liquefied butane out of the mixture before you start smoking it. Smoking butane is a bad idea in general so one wants to remove as much as possible.
- ✓ Cool the BHO.
- ✓ Break off a hit "half the size of a pinhead" and smoke it.
- ✓ Try to forget that you are inhaling a highly combustible gas, along with more THC than the world has ever seen, before using a blow torch to heat your needle (this part is easier than it sounds once the hit has been taken).

In essence, what has happened is that all of the THC in that trim, typically no less than an ounce, has been stripped out in liquid form.

Now that you understand the basics, check out a few videos online to really get it. One especially revealing video is entitled "Quick and Easy Way to Make BHO Wax" on YouTube by realkalilove, a "medical" cardholder from California. I love the part where he goes outside "for safety" and onto the patio next to the propane grill of his apartment community. Don't stop at my favorite, look around, there are plenty of videos to choose from, find your own fave!

Don't shut that browser just yet my friends, we're going to look at what happens when those less safety conscious than realkalilove make this stuff. Add one word, "explosion," to the end of your last search. If you are feeling extra hip and want to take this to the TLA (three letter acronym) world just search "BHO explosion."

Concentrates Are a Recipe for Disaster

I will start with a broad statement: concentrates have no place in the world and we shouldn't allow them to be sold in stores or manufactured by companies. Until we have a better idea of how this new drug interacts with users' brains and bodies, we need to hit the brakes and remind The Industry that just because we *can* do something doesn't mean we *should*. Because people, specifically lawmakers and state regulatory agencies, aren't paying attention to the details, concentrates are becoming prolific and are being pushed on consumers in an effort to expose users to a more potent and, therefore more addictive, high. Because we keep talking about weed like it's 1970, we are ignoring the rapid advances being made by The Industry, and unless we clamp down on it we will regret our inattention. Decriminalizing marijuana is one thing, creating a new substance, the effects of which we can't even imagine yet, then marketing and selling it out of stores *is just plain stupid*. Even if you are all for weed, and all for commercialized THC, we should all be outraged that this stuff is being sold as "weed" because it isn't. This product is a highly processed, manufactured hard drug that should be treated as such. For those of you who just got pissed that I called it a "hard drug" remember my credentials and compare them to yours when forming an opinion, or to the credentials of those telling you otherwise. I'm a recovering drug addict who knows a thing or two about weed/THC, I worked in a hospital-based treatment program in Colorado, and I pay very close attention to emerging trends because I am on the ground here and in the trenches. I am *not* an anti-drug warrior. I am also *not* someone trying to make money off this stuff. When you hear a softer version of what concentrates are, ask some questions about who is

talking. Is it The Lobby trying to soften the way you see commercialized THC? Is it someone who manufactures or sells this stuff who has
a vested financial interest in making it sound less harmful than it is?
Nobody I have ever spoken to who doesn't consume or stands to gain
financially or politically has defended concentrates.

In a recent interview in *The Cannabist*, (*The Denver Post's* specialty
publication dedicated to the cannabis culture) Ralph Morgan, the
CEO of OpenVape, said that smoking concentrates will soon be more
popular than smoking the plant leaves. He also said that more concentrates will be sold in Colorado in 2017 than plant form marijuana.
He goes on to say he "sees concentrates being a part of people's daily
regimen . . . you have vitamin A, vitamin B, vitamin C, I think we're
going to see vitamin CBD and vitamin THC as well being part of our
daily regimen as part of our health and well-being." He is advocating
the use of concentrates daily, for health. The article is called "Vape
CEO: Pot Concentrate Sales Will Soon Outpace Cannabis Flower."
There is even a video.

I hear all the time from people selling this crap that concentrates
are to weed what vodka is to wine. That makes my BS meter go off. It
is simply not true. Concentrates are to weed what crack is to a coca
plant. Put that on your hot knife and smoke it.

Enough is enough, we need to stop the manufacture and commercial sale of this substance right now before more people are hurt
as a result.

For those of you who want to follow the research side of this, there
is an interesting study taking place: cannabis-induced psychosis associated with high potency "wax dabs" [9] (Pierre/Gandal/Son).

---

9 http://www.sciencedirect.com/science/article/pii/S0920996416300561

Just for fun here are a few pictures advertising concentrates:

Snoop's private label concentrates

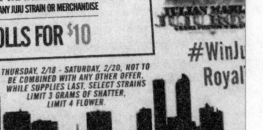
Getting cheaper!

Something for everyone, over 100 varieties!

Mix-and-match special.

That ounce of wax is worth more the farther one gets from
Colorado and is insanely easy to smuggle. The DEA in Florida
told me that it would be worth over $8,000 there.

95 percent THC, impressive!

Smoke wax, become a zombie!
Hey, you guys keep printing it, I will keep pointing it out.

Apparently, even Rudolph the Red-Nosed Reindeer is high on concentrates.

Even Fred Flinstone dabs! Throw in a couple of half-naked women
and we have an advertisment that appeals to kids of all ages.

First one is free! Seems to me I've heard that line somewhere else . . .

CHAPTER 6

Vaping

Get High Like a Ninja!

A conversation about vaping is important for many reasons. It's also fairly new on the scene, so there is little research out there, but we had better start talking now while we're waiting for the research findings. If we're not careful, I think some of the most devastating effects of marijuana use might come from people vaping. There are so many things about vaporizing THC that freak me out that it's kind of hard to know where to start.

Let's begin with the basics because I suppose there are those of you reading who don't know what handheld vaporizers are. These are little tools originally made to let people ingest nicotine without the tobacco or smoke. They use water vapor to create a steam that looks, and feels, like smoke while delivering the nicotine. It's just another delivery method to get some drug into the body. When vaporizers hit the market a few years ago they got traction pretty quickly. For one thing, they were advertised as cleaner than cigarettes—though they contain 4,000 chemicals mixed into the nicotine—and they didn't smell. You could even get them in different flavors. There are some major issues with them as a nicotine delivery system, but since this isn't a book about nicotine or cigarette companies we'll move onto the subject at hand: weed!

It was only a matter of time until the technology allowing nicotine to be delivered without a smell would be utilized for weed/THC. Not only did it happen quickly, but it's evolving much faster than the nicotine vapes did.

The THC vape pen manufacturing game is getting crowded now. Snoop Dog has his own line, so does 2 Chainz and a bunch of other people, but the innovation leaders still seem to be O.penVAPE. It's a cute play on words encouraging open consumption, right? You should see some of the campaigns they run, one that really stands out was the $10,000 giveaway where they encouraged customers to post pictures of themselves with their O.penVAPE pen. Not many of the shots were taken in private places.

O.penVAPE makes many different kinds of vaporizers for THC consumption but it all started with a little version that combusted and delivered THC in oil form. The oil came in little plastic packets, and some manufacturers made the pens to combust the plastic along with the oil, nasty! Pretty quickly, somebody—I think it was the "pro" designers Pinnacle—realized that with a few adjustments to temperature, a vape pen could also consume organic matter (weed) and concentrates.

All that was required was to bring the temperature down a bit for the flowers and get it up to above 700 degrees for the concentrates.

The necessary improvements happened pretty quickly. Vape pens today can combust THC or weed in just about any form and do it without leaving a smell. That's super good if you live in Colorado like me. In a way, I hope more people start using them so I have to smell less weed being burned every time I go downtown. But the innovation is bad news if you're a school resource officer, teacher, or other educator. If it's not bad enough that a student could be eating, chewing, sucking on or drinking THC right in front of you, now they can actually smoke (vape) it in class, if they're sneaky and slick enough, and get away with it.

I thought I was slick back in school, before things went way south for me. I went to a big high school, lots and lots of kids, and very crowded halls. They used to give us seven minutes between classes. That was a bad idea. It might not sound like a lot of time, but you can get in a lot of trouble in that amount of time. While it was easily enough time to sneak a cigarette in the bathroom, you couldn't make it outside to get high so I had another technique that worked well. I held whatever it was I was smoking in my thumb and index finger with the burning end pointed up into the palm of my hand. Since I always had a jacket on, I was able to bring my sleeve up to my mouth, take a drag, and then exhale the smoke back up my sleeve. Yes, I smelled pretty damn bad and got some odd looks, but I never once got caught.

I undoubtedly wasn't the only one who got high in school. Knowing what I now know, I can say that it likely didn't help my academic career much. We had a big security team at the high school I started at in Northern Virginia. When they were paying attention to someone, that person didn't get high as much because nobody wants to get caught with drugs in school. But vaporizers that combust THC with no odor change the entire equation. Now that kids *can* get away with it, I can guarantee that they *are* getting away with it.

We have been seeing a very disturbing trend recently. I should have seen this one coming but, honestly, it blindsided me.

Question: If a vaporizer can combust concentrates at 700-plus degrees what else can it combust?

A) Crack
B) Heroin
C) Meth
D) All of the above

Like any good multiple choice test-taker, you likely chose D. When you see it, "All of the above" is pretty much always a safe bet. Good job, D it is! This isn't necessarily the weed industry's fault, but without their influence there wouldn't be products this, um, tricky. I don't think they were trying to create a tool to smoke meth with no smell, but they did create or enhance a tool that works for all these substances. People can now combust what the world accepts as "hard drugs" in vape pens. I propose we change the way we look at hard drugs and say that if it needs to be "hot-knifed" or heated to over 700 degrees in order to be taken into somebody's body, it's a "hard drug." Seems like a solid working definition to me, I'm going with it.

A pretty smart guy once wrote, "There is nothing new under the sun." Correct me on this one if I'm wrong, but I'm pretty sure this *is* new territory. *Making drugs easier for people to use and for kids to get away with using them* is not *a good idea*. I'm also not sure that holding a stick up to my face that heats up to 700 degrees is a good idea, so I recommend we stay away from that scene.

THC-specific vapes are often hiding in plain sight. If you see kids with these things, call them out. If you see anyone with the "new and improved," 700-degree version, give them hell because that one is messed up.

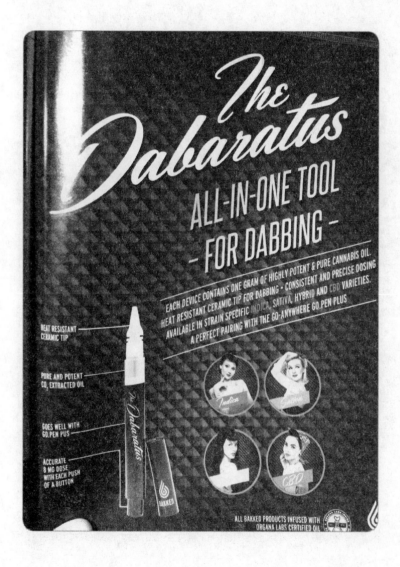

CHAPTER 7

Edibles

Brownies? That's so 1970s!

I've never had an "edible." I have, however, eaten weed. I had a couple of brownies back in the day. They tasted okay and got me kind of high, which I wanted, but they were also full of stems that got stuck in my teeth. It was like "surprise cake" that has candy baked into it; you never knew when a bite would turn into something more! I've also actually eaten weed, like really eaten it. Join me as I take a walk down memory lane.

The day had gotten off to a memorable start. It was a sunny summer day in Vienna, Virginia, and after scoring a decent amount of dope I was hanging out in the woods bordering a sports field off the bike trail. I had about $20 worth of weed with me when we left the trees to go back to our parked car; the rest was stashed or smoked. As we crossed the field, it quickly became obvious that we weren't alone.

Apparently, one of the parents at the kiddy soccer practice in a field nearby noticed the telltale smell and called the cops, who were in the parking lot clearly waiting for us.

It seemed obvious to me, at the time, what I had to do to avoid trouble. No weed, no evidence, no trouble. I emptied the bag inside of my pocket into my hand while also fishing out a cigarette. It was a pretty impressive move, as I recall, and made me think I should have been a magician. While bringing the smoke up to my mouth I popped the weed in first and then took the 200 or so yards to the parking lot trying to get it down the hatch while looking unconcerned and enjoying my Marlboro. Fortunately, my buddy had a gallon jug of water with him that I took a few long pulls from to help get it swallowed. By the time we made it to the car, we were just a couple of stoned kids who denied being stoned knowing that the only trouble we could get into was having our smokes taken because we were underage. We were searched, given a talking to and then let go. I felt pretty damn good; I'd outsmarted The Man. But as the day wore on I felt progressively less cool. The weed I ate started to punch back. It didn't happen quickly so I did what anyone in my frame of mind would do. I went back to my buddy's place and started to drink and smoke more weed. When I started to feel not so awesome I stopped smoking and drinking but couldn't stop my digestive system from processing that marijuana and THC, which lasted several hours. The details are fuzzy, but I recall it being a pretty rough afternoon.

I think those two examples do a good job of summing up edibles in the twentieth century. The rest of this chapter will explore what they look like in the twenty-first century, following commercialization.

Let's start with the good. After all, I've been a bit of a Debbie Downer thus far throughout the book, so something positive is in order. Edibles keep people from smoking! As we all know, smoking is bad, so consumers of THC edibles spare their lungs. Another plus, I have been told, is that many edibles (candies, desserts, sodas) taste *mmm-mmm* good!

Now that we have covered the advantages, I can get back to doing what I do, pointing out why The Industry sucks and what they are really doing on the street.

For multiple reasons, (cannabutter, concentrates, concentrated sprays, etc.) edibles aren't just about brownies anymore. They are made into and from everything: suckers, mints, caramels, chocolates, gummy bears, gummy worms, sour gummies, tarts, breath sprays, sodas, hot cocoa, hard candies, taffy, candy bars, coffee, ice cream, cotton candy, main course meals and side dishes. The list goes on and on. If you can eat it somebody has put THC into it and sold it in Colorado.

Some take name-brand candy—like Lemon Heads, Swedish Fish, and Sour Patch Kids—purchase them in bulk and then infuse and repackage them. The Denver police even had to put out a special message for parents around Halloween warning people to check their children's stash of goodies in case they ended up with THC-infused candy, which often looks identical.

Check it out "Keep out of reach from children." Okay, at least they warned us.

They say a picture is worth a thousand words, if that's true the following pictures of edibles could be a book in itself. You have to see this stuff to believe it.

Another reason to
be excited about the
holiday season

The Peppermint Bark Bar from BlueKudu
Layers of dark chocolate and white chocolate
with real peppermint bits and 100mg THC

$20

100mg THC Gummies

Highly Edible products are
organic, vegan, THC-infused fruit
gummies from the makers of the
popular CannaPunch.

$6

I think 20 legal servings in one gummy is a new record,
but give it a minute it won't stand for long.

Because The Industry has fought so hard to avoid stamping their products as containing THC, it hasn't happened yet. I was recently asked at a talk how one could tell the difference between a THC-infused gummy bear and a regular gummy bear. The best I can tell you is that much of the time the gummy bear infused with THC is rolled in sugar before being repackaged and sold; other than that, there is little way to tell.

So now that we know what they look like, it's time to understand what they do. Simply put, they get you high. How high depends on lots of things; how much THC they contain, how quickly you consume them, what your tolerance is, what else you have eaten and the size of your body, a lot like alcohol, actually. Where they differ from alcohol is in the amount of time they take to go to your brain and how long the effects last. Edibles are also more unpredictable and most importantly, consumed solely with the intent of getting high. I know plenty of people who have a drink and don't intend to get drunk, I have yet to meet a person who eats an edible without the intention of achieving some level of intoxication. Depending on the variables above and a few others, an edible can induce a subtle effect or pack a wicked punch.

After visiting Colorado to report on the start of legal recreational marijuana in the state, Maureen Dowd wrote an op-ed piece in *The New York Times* entitled, "Don't Harsh Our Mellow, Dude." In it, she describes a frightening episode of THC overdose she had after eating a THC-infused candy bar that was pretty intense and lasted for over eight hours, "What could go wrong with a bite or two? Everything, as it turned out." Dowd was not alone in her experience. As she discovered when she interviewed Andrew Freedman, at the time the state's director of marijuana coordination, "There are way too many stories of people not understanding how much they're eating. . . . It would behoove The Industry to create a more pleasant experience for people." What Ms. Dowd missed here, however, is that The Industry doesn't target her and other casual users nearly as much as they do the dedicated users who want as much THC as they can get.

People who eat edibles are the "pot poisonings" hospitals talk about when they report numbers. The physical effects won't kill you (in all but rare cases causing a spike in blood pressure), but combined with the psychedelic effects they sure can freak you out! Most people who come to the emergency room for pot are there because the edible hit too hard. Their extreme high turned into paranoia or a psychotic episode, landing them in the ER. I'm going to get to some specific examples of when edibles are more dangerous than that and what can happen when things go *really* wrong after eating them, but not yet; you have to understand a few things first.

Serving Size

We didn't have a long time to build the regulatory infrastructure for commercialized THC in Colorado before retail rolled out. The vote was certified at the end of 2012 and commercial sales started January 1, 2014. The regulations had to be done in June 2013, so the entire complex infrastructure had to be built in only six months. Because of this reality (solid planning when writing the law by The Lobby), much was left undone and had to be figured out later—and much of it influenced by The Industry. One of the things we got right was limiting how much THC could be put into an edible, settling on 10 milligrams. I would like to have seen 5 milligrams per serving, but it was a decent compromise. Edibles would only have 10 milligrams of THC in them, or so we thought. As it turns out, we were totally sucker punched. What we were talking about wasn't what The Industry was talking about. They viewed 10 milligrams per serving as no limit because they would put as much THC as they could into products and then say that they contained multiple servings. There are some unbelievable examples we will get into, but nothing sums it up better than the gummy bears. The majority of THC gummy bears in Colorado contain 40 milligrams of THC *in each one*. Not four servings per bag, or even one serving per bear, but *four times the legal limit in each gummy bear!* Because we are chumps we continue to let them put four, and as many as twenty, servings in a gummy bear, and they tell the public that it's their duty to cut that gummy bear into fourths or twentieths and "consume responsibly." Seriously, they do that, and we are letting them. The Industry does this because it's in their nature; they must maximize profit. The issue is that our frog of a state government keeps offering rides across the stream to the Industry scorpion no matter how many times we get stung. People are actually dying because we won't stop this nonsense, and we don't seem to care. We let them do what they want and look the other way. Come on Colorado, let's wise up a little bit, nobody cuts gummy bears into fourths, nobody. The Food and Drug Administration doesn't let this kind of deception happen with food products, but they can't touch these products, as I'll explain in detail later, because they are federally illegal.

Another great example is Cheeba Chews. These taffy-like, Jolly Rancher-sized candies are a potent form of THC ingestion. When this product first came out, it had as much as in their "deca-dose" product; 100 milligrams of THC in each piece of candy, 10 legal servings per piece. They now advertise 175 milligrams of THC per serving, 17.5

servings per piece. Why do they do this? Simply because they can. These little candies come in flavors like chocolate, caramel, green hornet, orange, etc. *High Times* magazine endorsed them as, "Potent, Consistent, Discreet." The manufacturers are smart, pushing the limits of how much THC can be crammed into a small candy. They actually have a little warning on the package saying, "Danger: Extremely Potent." News flash: nobody cuts a Jolly Rancher-sized taffy into 17 parts, but the shrewd marketing guys at Cheeba Chews know that.

You know what else people don't do? No one drinks 1/35th of a soda. That's apparently not a problem for the folks producing Keef Cola with 350 milligrams of THC per bottle. This sugary, carbonated beverage seriously has thirty-five legal servings in each bottle, and

I'm not much of a math guy, but I'm pretty sure that comes out to 2,100 mgs of THC for $36. That's almost six servings for $1. If you are trying to get high that math works! But is that responsible regulation?

you can get a bottle for $10. With a coupon, you can get 40 percent off, but you're limited to six bottles . . . *in each flavor!*

Multiple servings in one goodie is a mistake. If we were serious about regulating these guys rather than placating them, we would never allow this nonsense. Imagine if the nutritional information on a container of Oreos represented that each bag contained two servings. We would feel pretty good about bingeing on Oreos because they would appear healthy unless one read the fine print. For those of you in the states considering marijuana legislation, ask your lawmakers not to cave into The Industry standards and require that one serving actually is *one serving.*

You've seen the pictures of commercially sold edibles in Colorado and are probably asking yourself how they made those gummy bears look so much like real gummy bears. The answer is simple: "repurposing."

The Industry calls it "repurposed" candy because that sounds better than saying what it actually is: an innocent-looking and powerful means to get high. The THC gummy bears are actually gummy bears purchased in bulk, sprayed with a concentrated THC, rolled in sugar and then repackaged, and often described as "medicine." The fact that we are allowing this to happen further demonstrates the insanity surrounding much of the legislation around THC in this country. They are actually Lemon Drops that are turned into a highly potent drug and then resold! You thought candy cigarettes were bad, imagine doing this kind of manufacturing and marketing with any other substance: nicotine-infused Pop-Tarts, alcohol-infused gummies, and codeine-infused sodas. We would never stand for this kind of crap, but since it's weed (or so we have been led to believe) we look the other way—*and this is absolutely disgraceful.*

Candy Edibles Aren't Sweet:
Some Tragic Stories

On April 15, 2014, Richard Kirk went down to his local dispensary and picked up some THC. He purchased a pre-rolled joint and a Karma Candy—a little treat with 100 milligrams of THC in it. He ate the THC candy on his way home and got extremely high. As this story unfolds, bear in mind that toxicology reports later showed nothing else in his system other than THC. Let's also keep in mind that this is a horrible tragedy and I'm not telling the story lightly. I went back and forth a bunch deciding if it should be included. Bottom line is that this stuff happens, and unless we consider the tragedies along with the "advantages" we can't make an informed decision about policy.

After Richard got home, things got really bad. In all likelihood, he experienced THC-induced psychosis, a condition we are seeing more and more of in Colorado. He started ranting and jumping in and out of windows. Kristen, his terrified wife, called police because their three children were in the house and Richard was talking about the end of the world and how he wanted Kristen to shoot him. The entire episode was recorded since she was talking with 911 for much of the time. While she was waiting for the police to arrive, and still on the phone with the dispatcher, Richard pulled their handgun out of the safe and shot her in the head. Their youngest son, who was only seven years old at the time, watched his mother die.

Richard originally plead not guilty, then not guilty by reason of insanity. He later changed his plea to guilty of second-degree murder, agreeing to serve twenty-five to thirty years in prison and relinquishing custody of his children.

The three boys (through their grandparents, who are their guardians) brought what is thought to be the country's first wrongful-death complaint against a recreational marijuana company, Gaia's Gardens, and its distributor, Nutritional Elements. A direct quote from the lawsuit states:

The company "negligently, recklessly and purposefully concealed vital dosage and labeling information from their actual and prospective purchasers, including Kirk, to make a profit."

Also, according to the lawsuit, the label on the candy purportedly contained 101 milligrams of THC, far above the 10 milligram single-serving recommendation. The children are seeking damages for negligence, failure to warn, wrongful death, deceptive trade, strict liability, breach of implied warranty, misrepresentation, and consumer law violations.

On March 11, 2014, Levy Thamba Pongi, a nineteen-year-old foreign exchange student from the Democratic Republic of Congo, came to Colorado for spring break. An engineering student at Northwest College in Powell, Wyoming, Pongi certainly could have gone spring skiing closer to his campus, and Denver isn't otherwise a mecca for spring breakers who would typically rather go hit the beach somewhere. Levi and his friends chose Colorado for an obvious reason: to get high, that was their plan. You might be scratching your head thinking, *Wait, this kid was underage. How did they score THC?* Impossible as it may be to conceive, our tightly regulated market is hardly that. These kids checked into a hotel in Denver—as do many pot tourists—and started to party. Levy had never had marijuana before in any form, and he ate a chocolate chip cookie with 80 milligrams of THC—eight legal servings.

Wisely at first, and unlike most others, he consumed an eighth of the cookie. But then, like so many others, when it didn't affect him quickly, he consumed the remaining 70 milligrams. The behavior that followed makes many think this was also likely psychosis from the THC. Levy's friends report that he started acting wild, running around the room, pulling pictures off the wall, and punching holes in things. Unfortunately, the night turned deadly. Levi ran out onto the balcony and jumped off, falling to his death. The coroner cited marijuana intoxication as the cause of death. This nineteen-year-old kid with a wide-open future, a kid who came from a war-torn country, met a horrible end in the land of peace and prosperity. A kid who chose something he was told for years was harmless and that had never killed anyone. He ended up losing his life as a result of eating one cookie.

Twenty-three-year-old Luke Goodman drove out to Colorado with his family from Tulsa, Oklahoma, to ski at Keystone the spring of 2015. Like Richard and Levy, Luke had no history of mental illness or related issues. He was a young guy who had graduated from college and was hanging out with his family in one of the prettiest places in the country. A few days into the trip Luke and his cousin Caleb decided to take a rest day. They took a bus to nearby Silverthorne and visited one of the local dispensaries—one of sixteen in the county composed of small resort towns. There, they purchased $78 worth of edibles and marijuana including some THC-infused peach rings. The young men anticipated a fun afternoon and Caleb said of Luke, "He was excited to do them."

When they got back to Keystone, Luke ate one of the peach rings—one is considered a serving—but apparently he didn't feel it enough so he ate four more, including two at one time. In all, Luke ingested five times the recommended amount. Luke's mother said they likely didn't see the warning on the back of the package saying that "the intoxicating effects of this product may be delayed by two or more hours." The psychotic episode that followed was described in detail to authorities by his cousin Caleb. Luke became "pretty weird and relatively incoherent. It was almost like something else was speaking through him." The family left the condo for the evening but Luke would not join them. While they were out, he retrieved a handgun from the car and shot himself in the head.

These deaths are just a few in a growing list of tragedies associated with THC consumption. Sadly, these accounts were almost totally ignored by the media. *But let one person say that marijuana makes their headache go away and CNN will trip over Fox to get them on tape telling the story.* The *whole* story deserves to be told. Bad things do happen with THC.

I know what it's like to lose family. If I could, I'd like to offer my sincere apologies to the families of those who died in these stories for my state's reckless policies. I believe they led to these tragic losses of life. They all remain in my prayers.

FDA Issues

The FDA is a federal, not a state, agency. *This is a big deal.* The fact that the FDA is a federal agency is critically important to understanding why the marijuana industry seems to be operating in the days of the Wild West instead of our modern times with its strict regulatory guidelines and consumer protection standards. **Since marijuana/ THC is illegal federally, a federal agency can't have anything to do with it, including helping to "regulate" it. Doing so would put them at direct odds with the federal law, therefore they can't.** The ramifications of this are enormous. The agency that keeps our food and drugs safe can't regulate this rapidly growing industry. When you consider that states have very little in the way of regulatory agencies in place to do these jobs, the lack of involvement by the FDA makes the situation even scarier. Everybody who goes on about marijuana being the same as beer should consider that beer production is governed by federal law, and it's been doing this job for many years.

To further make my case let's use a food analogy. Consider this very real scenario: I want to open a cookie shop. I'm going to bake, package, and sell cookies. It's going to be awesome! Before it can be awesome, before I can take anything to market, heck, before I can even start baking I'll need to be in compliance with about a million federal regulations. This is good news for those of you who will eventually be eating my cookies. You wouldn't want to end up with a bunch of stuff in there that would make you sick! You would want the peace of mind that comes with knowing that decades of thought, legislation, and lawsuits have gone into creating the consumer protections we have in place to make sure that people don't get sick or die from eating a bad cookie. My cookie has to be created in a way that minimizes any risk to the consumers. And if I do end up hurting people who eat the cookies, I will get sued out of existence and the people and families will split the class-action winnings.

Now, let's say I don't feel like screwing with all of this FDA stuff. I want to make what I want to make and sell it how I feel like selling it. It's simple; all I do is add THC to my cookie and bye-bye FDA. Because my now THC-infused cookie is illegal federally you can't see me, you can't regulate me, and you can't sue me! Gotcha, Feds, with your overzealous FDA. I'll make whatever I feel like making—and sell it!

It should be easy to see how we have gotten into the mess we now have in Colorado, including recent episodes of pesticide residue turning up in THC foods and candies. As of this writing, the state's

Marijuana Enforcement Division (MED) has issued dozens of recalls covering well over 100,000 pieces of food that have been infused with THC by this industry.

Let's recap what has been presented so far about edibles:

✓ They affect users in ways that they are not always ready for.

✓ They can come with up to thirty-five legal servings in one item. I'd bet this number could be much higher by the time this book goes to press.

✓ They come in forms that are limited only by the imagination of those selling them.

✓ Many are clearly created to appeal to kids.

✓ Their use can, and has, been lethal.

✓ It's hard to say just what is in them because nobody is regulating them except those who manufacture them. (Remember the fox guarding the henhouse?)

Of all the THC being sold in Colorado, edibles make up 40 percent of the market. Please tell me I'm not the only person who sees a problem with this! When the theoretical meets the actual, this is what it looks like with THC.

The world now has a model to look to in Colorado. We need to ask what's working and what isn't working, then filter out the politicians who are trying to look good managing it and The Industry trying to get in your wallet. *Let's apply simple common sense when talking about edibles.* If we actually start doing this we'd likely see the end of THC candy and dozens of servings in one snack. If this doesn't seem like common sense to you, you're probably a kid or someone selling this stuff. Because I care for the futures of the former I have little sympathy for the frustration of the latter.

CHAPTER 8

Weed and the Environment

There Is Nothing "Green" About This Stuff

The culture around weed is different than other drugs, in many ways. One of the ways it differs from, say, meth is that it is "just a plant" and attracts people who dig plants more than highly processed drugs that are destructive to their bodies and the environment. Do you see where I'm going with this?

In decades past, people grew a little weed and they grew it in climates and locations favorable for its cultivation. Northern California was a hotbed, as was Mexico, the Caribbean, and other similar places. There were issues, of course, when drug cartels would take over public land for big grow operations and poison the ground and water with fertilizers and pesticides. Fortunately, those were few and far between. Weed farmers shipped out some of their crop to places like Colorado, for instance, so people could get high. Growing a few plants in the back yard garden has been the norm for generations. But things have changed.

We're going to look at several areas of environmental concern in this chapter but it basically boils down to a few things:

- ✓ Pot doesn't grow naturally in many of the places we are growing it.
- ✓ This giant industry has no environmental safeguards.
- ✓ Weed is water and power hungry.
- ✓ Many commercial growers don't give a crap about anything other than the bottom line.

I believe that some of what follows will be a big enough shock that even dedicated users will second guess their support for commercialization. We are doing so little to protect resources for future generations to begin with, and it blows my mind that so many people who are in tune with the environmental movement can so easily endorse commercially produced THC. Some priorities need closer scrutiny.

A number of recent studies/reports on this topic have seemed to fly totally under the world's radar. It's time to start looking at this issue from all sides to determine if this is the direction we *really* want to go as a country. How so many people can turn a blind eye to the damage we are doing at so many levels is nuts.

The Obama administration did much to improve our environment but if current and future administrations aren't careful, this issue could erase the gains made elsewhere. Driving a hybrid is good but putting an end to thoughtless and damaging corporate practices is better. The impact we are having on our planet by allowing commercial THC to go unchecked is real, and if you choose to support

The Industry you should know what you're doing. We're talking about establishing another huge industry, like tobacco and alcohol, that will always put profits ahead of the community and the planet. Because there is so much money to be made, it will not take limitations lying down.

Water

First things first, Southern California was in the middle of a major drought when I started writing this book. I travel to this region a few times a year for work and was there during the time when there were major water restrictions in place. While many states have lawn-watering restrictions, the drought had reached such a critical stage that they even had showering regulations. It was a bit of a personal challenge to do the sub-three-minute shower they recommended for residents when I visited. It's harder than it sounds. Basically, you can't wait for the water to get hot or you've already wasted precious time (and water) so you hop in cold and get wet, then you kill the water. You lather up and get your hair all shampooed then turn the water back on to rinse off. Fortunately, the last hotel I was in had awesome hot water so I was totally warm by the rinse—but that wasn't always the case! While inconvenient, these kinds of regulations are absolutely necessary in such an arid environment and during those extraordinary conditions. Last year, I was there when they stopped giving out water at restaurants unless you specifically asked for it. Signs were posted everywhere saying how water was being conserved; it was kind of wild. There were actually stores springing up that sold turf grass because the watering restrictions were so severe that it was impossible to grow a lawn. They even had some kind of 1984-esque water reporting hotline where you could turn your neighbors in for wasting water!

California also has the second largest commercial weed industry in the country (after Colorado of course) and it's centered in Southern Cal. While the old hippie pot farmers grew their weed in Northern California, the commercial business is now mostly in the South. Californians love their weed but weed *loves* water. It is a very thirsty plant that consumes a ton of water. I spent a long time looking over grow sites and even a few official reports and people swear different things so there is a lot of variation in what people say weed uses. While one wants to be careful when the plant is young not to over water, when it is mature, the average weed plant probably uses between two and five liters of water each day. Compared with human consumption, The Institute of Medicine says that an average adult male needs to drink about three liters of water a day. While the science isn't exact I like the simplicity of considering each weed plant growing in California as another person sucking water up, it's a good visual. Considering that there are huge grow operations that house hundreds of thousands of plants in one warehouse, let's stop for a second to consider where the good people of California have allowed their priorities to be placed:

As a Coloradan, I get how it must feel for the people who were there in the days of pre-industrial weed. They are living in a different world now, one that gives more attention to getting high than showering.

There is plenty to read on this subject if you're interested. Start with the article written by Brittany Patterson published in *Scientific American* in July 2015 entitled, "Sucking Rivers Dry." For those of you somewhat familiar with weed in America, you know that Humboldt County, in coastal Northern California, is a historical pot-growing community that boasts some of the best weed on Earth. It's a pretty big part of the culture there. In one article, county native and sheriff Tom Allman is quoted as saying, "Old hippies are not the problem, the problem is twenty-year-olds with a sore shoulder who want to make $1 million a year." He is, of course, referencing California's "medical" marijuana market because that's all they have there, at the time of this writing. Recreational retail sales begin on January 1, 2018.

Back in 2010, the Public Broadcasting Service (PBS) ran a story called, "Pot: Not So Green After All?" It reported that 1,000 gallons of diesel fuel had spilled into one stream alone from a pot grow.

In a study published in the journal *Bioscience* on July 15, 2014, entitled, "High Time for Conservation: Adding the Environment to the Debate on Marijuana Liberalization," the authors discuss water issues in detail:

> The liberalization of marijuana policies, including the legalization of medical and recreational marijuana, is sweeping the United States and other countries. Marijuana cultivation can have significant negative collateral effects on the environment that are often unknown or overlooked. Focusing on the state of California, where by some estimates 60 percent–70 percent of the marijuana consumed in the United States is grown, we argue that (a) the environmental harm caused by marijuana cultivation merits a direct policy response, (b) current approaches to governing the environmental effects are inadequate, and (c) neglecting discussion of the environmental impacts of cultivation when shaping future marijuana use and possession policies represents a missed opportunity to reduce, regulate, and mitigate environmental harm.

I couldn't agree more with them when they say that the environmental harm merits a direct policy response. If we are going to move in this direction let's not miss the opportunity to make The Industry play by the same rules that everyone else must follow, and to tell this side of the story to voters before asking them to decide on the future of their state by relying on sound bites created and written by The Industry.

Power

According to a study published in the journal *Energy Policy* in 2012[10], growing weed takes upwards of 1 percent of the energy produced in the United States. Keep in mind, this was before commercialization here in Colorado, and in a few other states where they were basically just talking about underground and "medical" weed. The study also finds that for every kilogram of weed produced in the United States, an estimated 4,600 kilograms of carbon dioxide is released into the environment. Burning one liter of diesel fuel releases about 2.6 kilograms of carbon; that works out to 1,769 liters of diesel fuel burned for every kilo of weed.

Xcel Energy is the largest supplier of power to Colorado, producing about 60 percent of the power sold in the state. In August 2014, their spokesman was quoted as saying that legal grows were consuming .5 to 1 percent of all of the power generated in the state, again, this is before the commercial market really exploded. The reasons *why* it is so intensive are simple. Allowing plants to grow around the clock means they can be taken to market faster. We're back to the money! To grow around the clock, one must use really intense lights that get

---

10 "The Carbon Footprint of Indoor Cannabis Production," Evan Mills, March, 17, 2012.

very, very hot. To mitigate that heat, grows need fans and ventilation systems to clear all of that hot air out of their warehouses. All of those things use power—and lots of it.

If we had an infinite supply of power in the world this wouldn't be a big issue; the growers will pay for the power use, and everyone would be happy. As with everything, it's not quite that simple. Power has to be made somehow. In Colorado we get two-thirds of our power by burning coal and another 20 percent from burning natural gas. That means that 86 percent of our power is created by burning non-renewable resources—things that we can't get back—and that are bad for the environment because they release greenhouse-causing gasses. Is growing weed the best use of those finite resources?

Like many of you, I am eagerly awaiting the power consumption data from post industrialization. Unless I'm way off the mark, those numbers will be pretty sobering for those of us who are concerned with the well-being of the environment.

Pesticides

Unfortunately, but not surprisingly, much of the environmental impact from commercially grown weed has been kept under wraps. However, what has been particularly frightening in Colorado are all of the state-issued recalls over pesticides found in THC products. As explained earlier, because we can't rely on the federal government for help, we are left to figure this stuff out on our own. Consequently, I'm sure that plenty is falling between the cracks. Even with that said, this has been a huge issue and gets plenty of press in Colorado.

It's pretty obvious why using pesticides in the production of weed—a plant being grown for people to eat, drink, and smoke—is a bad idea. *Chemicals that are bad for our bodies to touch are even worse for our bodies to ingest or inhale.*

Clearly, there is an issue using products that are banned by the FDA to grow potted plants in the cultivation of weed. Maybe the easiest way to elaborate about this would be to give you the list of products that have been recalled in Colorado recently because they tested positive for banned pesticides. While I would love to do that, the list is just too long and wouldn't fit anywhere nice, so here is a quick sample:

- ✓ Mountain High Suckers recalled 99,574 pieces of THC candy in December 2015.
- ✓ Open Vape recalled an "undetermined" amount of individual units including a few fun strains like Crack Dawg and Cherry Durban Poison.
- ✓ Advanced Medical Alternatives had to recall a bunch of wax because it was full of banned pesticides.
- ✓ EdiPure had to recall 32,125 individual units of approximately 23 different gummy and hard candy products including such favorites as Rainbow Belts, Orange Cream Licorice, Sour Gummy Bears, and Cherry Bombs

The list goes on as long as one would care to search, but my favorite has to be from The Farm. This Boulder-based manufacturer is all about doing "craft cannabis" organically and well.

As we are about to learn, The Farm isn't pesticide-free as advertised on the next page, kinda makes me wonder how gluten-free it actually is. Is the definition of gluten-free being used here the FDA standard of the definition, or just a familiar phrase we assume to be true as natural and healthy?

Craft cannabis, not exactly pesticide-free

In a recent recall, The Farm was forced to recall sixteen batches of marijuana that tested positive for ivermectin and thirty-six batches of the "headquarter" strain of cannabis that tested positive for spiromesifen. The product in the first recall contains something called ivermectin that is used to kill head lice and scabies. Spiromesifen is used to control a few pests in "ornamental plants," not things you typically smoke. The good people at The Farm, who are so committed to your health and the environment, just got busted spraying their weed with banned pesticides. You can't make this stuff up!

Although there are some exceptions, from what I can tell society as a whole has gotten smarter when it comes to realizing our environmental impact and the importance of protecting our planet and our scarce natural resources. As a result, laws are changing and, more importantly, our habits are changing as well. We ask questions about how our food is grown and prepared, we walk and bike when we can, and are actually paying attention to our power usage as well as our fuel consumption. But then along comes weed. We seem to be so enamored with the idea of commercialized weed that we haven't stopped to ask if what we are doing is good for society, our bodies, or the planet. Maybe those are a few of the areas we should consider more closely in the future.

CHAPTER 9

Law Enforcement

What's Johnny Law Saying?

Organized Crime

There are a few things I have decided that I can definitely count on in life, other than that old "death and taxes" bit. Here's a partial list: my kids will start getting excited for Christmas well before Halloween; the Broncos will always be good enough to break our hearts (unless of course we are talking about the 2015-16 season in which we proved to be *the best team in the NFL*); I will never understand how the game of cricket is scored; and at every talk I give, someone will pontificate, under the guise of asking a question, about how much the cartels suck and how marijuana legalization will fix those criminal bastards!

Were that true, were the organized crime issue *that* simple to fix, I would be at the front of the parade in my "Legalize It!" shirt and I would maybe be a card-carrying NORML, SAFER, and DPA member. *Unfortunately, the reality is much more complex.* Depending on what study you look at, between 7 and 20 percent of the cartels' revenue is generated from selling marijuana. For whatever someone wants to say about drug cartels, never let it be said that they don't know how to make money. They make money—lots and lots of money—and they will not write off any loss to their bottom line because we change some drug laws. I'm pretty sure that El Chapo's guys aren't going to go out and get jobs at KFC if the world legalizes weed. They will find new ways to get paid and they will be very good at it. Selling marijuana across the border has always baffled me a bit when there are so many other ways to get us to hand our dollars over, many with less stress on their end. Prices of weed fluctuate wildly depending on geography, potency, and quantity in which it's sold. For the most part, a pound of Mexican weed has a street value of $650, but Colorado weed costs $2,000 a pound. Compare that with a pound of meth for $7,000, a pound of processed cocaine at $14,700, and a pound of heroin going for $12,500. So why would the cartels ever go to the trouble of smuggling tons of weed into the United States instead of using that space for more profitable substances? This has always baffled me—until I realized that weed might be a really good way to get people more comfortable with using "harder" drugs.

It wasn't six months into Colorado's "experiment" that news stories started showing up telling us how marijuana fields south of the border were being rapidly repurposed to grow poppies for heroin. More heroin isn't good. Lots of people die from consuming too much, including many of my friends.

So long as there is a thirst for drugs there will be those willing to supply those drugs no matter the harm caused, the lives lost, and the cost to society. There are some who believe that this truth means we should throw in the towel and commercialize it all. Ethan Nadelmann, founder and executive director at the DPA, is very frank, "Let's stop pretending we want a drug-free society! Drugs are here to stay." That kind of nihilism scares me and defies simple logic. Carry that logic over to almost any other example and the ridiculousness is exposed. "People will always speed, what's the use of speed limits?" "We can't stop people from stealing cars, so why not make car theft legal?" "People will smoke cigarettes/meth/crack, so why try to stop them? Let's legalize it, tax it, and we'll all benefit!" We have made amazing progress combating cigarette smoking, not because we said, "Screw it, smokers are gonna smoke!" but because we made people aware of the very real health issues, fought the perception that it wasn't harmful, and stigmatized its use. How many teenagers do you see sneaking cigarettes these days? Likely not many. It's not cool anymore—and that's a great thing. Fewer people smoking means cheaper healthcare for all of us, definitely cleaner air and workplaces, and sidewalks, beaches, and parks not quite as littered with cigarette butts.

That logic holds perfectly true with drugs. If we *really* want to hit the cartels where it will hurt, I know how. We don't need the army or CIA, machine guns or grenades, informants and border patrol. We need to consume fewer drugs in America. Were we to move away from the idea that intoxication is the norm, that drug use is a forgone conclusion, that we can't possibly do anything about our appetite to get high, much would change. We need to be willing to take a hard look inside instead of pointing fingers "out there." Soon we would find that every time we get wasted we strengthen their position, we give them power. Consider that the next time you light up. Your drug use, at any level, makes cartels stronger.

We live in an age when being intoxicated is becoming the status quo. When massive advertising campaigns are being run to normalize a drug-induced state of mind. It's no longer something that is done in a celebratory manner with friends. Getting wasted is becoming "the new normal," and the cartels are laughing all the way to the bank!

I can be more passionate about this subject than most others, but I'll wait to close the chapter out with that soapbox.

In November 2013, forty-nine-year-old Hector Diaz was arrested at his $1.3 million home in an affluent area of metro Denver following raids focused on ten other Colombians tied to cartels who were running fifteen grow houses.

In 2015, a bunch of illegal grows were busted in national forests and state lands—you know, the place we go camping with our kids. These were also run by gangs from south of the border. Thanks to Fox 31 Denver for the story and summary.

Pike National Forest, August 19, in the Green Mountain Area in Jefferson County. Investigation is ongoing.

Law Enforcement Officers from the U.S. Forest Service, Department of Homeland Security Investigations (HSI), Jefferson County Sheriff's Office and the Colorado National Guard Joint Counter Drug Task Force joined together to complete an eradication of an illegal marijuana grow site in the Pike National Forest. The eradication team collected more than 3,900 plants and over 3,000 pounds of irrigation pipe, pesticides, flammable liquids, camping gear, and trash.

Pike National Forest, August 19 in the Green Mountain Area in Jefferson County. Investigation is ongoing.

Law Enforcement Officers from the U.S. Forest Service, U.S. Immigration and Customs Enforcement (ICE), Homeland Security

Investigations (HSI) and the Routt County Sheriff's Office joined together to eradicate an illegal marijuana grow site located in the Buffalo Pass area, northeast of Steamboat Springs. The eradication team collected approximately 1,000 plants and removed camping gear from the site. Further, a handgun was found. Additional site clean-up of trash and other items will be ongoing by the U.S. Forest Service. Two Mexican nationals in the country illegally were arrested.

Private Land, September 1, Cotopaxi and Westcliffe in Freemont and Custer County. 20 people arrested.

A DEA-led task force executed eight search warrants in Cotopaxi and Westcliffe as part of a major drug trafficking organization investigation. Agents and officers found well over 1,000 marijuana plants, 50 pounds of dried marijuana, 28 firearms, and $25,000 in cash. The investigation and seizures resulted ultimately in the arrest of 20 individuals, many from Cuba, acting in an organized manner according to investigators. Those arrested were growing the marijuana in Cotopaxi and Westcliffe, and then either driving or using UPS to get it to Florida.

San Isabel National Forest, September 7, Cordova Pass Area northwest of Trinidad in Huerfano County, two arrested.

Hunters discovered an illegal marijuana grow site located in the Cordova Pass area approximately 40 miles northwest of Trinidad. The eradication team collected more than 11,700 plants as well as irrigation pipe, pesticides, flammable liquids, camping gear and trash. The U.S. Forest Service and Huerfano County Sheriff's Office are working together to identify the individuals. The cultivation site spread across 10 acres with some of the growing areas above 10,000 feet in elevation. The overall grow area included a kitchen structure, three sleeping areas and a rifle. Two men were arrested at one of the campsites within the cultivation area.

Bureau of Land Management land, September 15, along the Dolores River corridor between Gateway and Naturita in Montrose County, four arrested.

BLM Rangers discovered more than 1,200 fully mature marijuana plants, many exceeding six feet tall, along with 211 kilograms of dried marijuana and a rifle. Because of the size of the operation, officers spent two-and-a-half days eradicating and removing the plants. The rangers arrested four Mexican nationals who were on-scene and believed to be working the grow site.

Bureau of Land Management land, September 30, also along the Dolores River corridor between Gateway and Naturita in Montrose County, six arrested.

Law enforcement officers identified a marijuana grow site, also along the Dolores River. Evidence of at least 1,000 marijuana plants appeared recently harvested with approximately 69.6 kilograms of processed marijuana still on site. The rangers arrested one Honduran and five Mexican nationals at or near the site.

The reality is that we have beaten the border crossing for them! Why in the world would they risk losing product and incurring the added expense of getting weed from Mexico into the U.S. when Colorado's borders aren't protected? These cartel growers exist in the "gray" market that has been created since legalization. We are awash in weed, growing massive quantities with impunity and shipping it out from here. That's why there were eighty-eight filings regarding weed under the Colorado Organized Crime Control Act between 2012 and 2015. I'm not the best business man in the world—just ask my wife—but I know enough to tell you that we have hung a great big green "help wanted" sign at our southern border. We have communicated very clearly to the cartels: We love getting high up here, come help us! We have also given them a place to launder their money that has to be second to none. In our all-cash free-for-all industry we are awash in Benjamins. We aren't going to solve the banking issue that keeps any money made selling weed, even in a "legal" market, illegal for the bank to accept anytime soon, so the THC business will continue to operate on the fringes of our financial system. With that much cash flying around why not set up shop in Colorado to wash the money you earn selling other drugs, extorting families of kidnapping victims, and running guns? We have given them a place where huge amounts of cash that smell like drugs are the norm and where they have lobbyists working to get that money into the established financial system.

Many of our dispensaries are openly advertising that they take credit cards. In fact, I once used a credit card to purchase edibles to prove a point before a talk a friend was giving in Colorado. Those credit cards can't be accepted for the sale of THC; it's illegal, so they have to be dummy corporations. If you own a weed shop and want to take my Amex, you will have to run it through a legal business. I'm guessing that these dispensaries take cash for their THC and run the credit cards through front corporations, maybe a lawn service or something. I'll bet they get a good laugh each time they run a credit card for "grass services" and the customer walks out the door with an ounce of infused gummy bears.

Let's take a break from organized crime and look at what's going on with law enforcement as it pertains to weed. I do a bunch of training and speaking to police all over the country and the mood seems to be pretty universal: it's not happy. While you might think that they'd have to spend less time worrying about weed because it is now legal, the opposite is actually true. Because the commercialized THC scene is changing so quickly, they can hardly keep up with all of the demands on them to enforce existing laws while learning new ones.

I know a bunch of cops in all different divisions: uniformed officers, vice, highway patrol, and administrative brass. Not one of them has ever told me that they locked people up for smoking weed. Nobody was kicking doors in to bust Grandma eating a brownie or Uncle Whoever burning one down. Most law enforcement hasn't cared about personal use for years. Someone found in possession of two ounces or less; received a simple citation in Colorado pre-A64. And while we can, of course, find examples of instances contrary to that statement, it holds true the vast majority of the time. For all of the talk about freeing up their time so they can focus on "real crime" all we have done is bog them down in weed-related violations, such as trafficking and illegal grows, making it harder to focus on anything else. One new expense has been to retire the drug dogs in the state (can't un-train a dog to smell something). These dogs were trained to sniff out all drugs, but now if they hit on weed, anything they discover is not legally "discoverable." Because of this, they have to train up a whole new batch of dogs—not cheap, from what I understand. The most ironic part of all this is that legalization laws made sure none of the tax money collected from weed sales went to help defer those costs. Municipalities are having to pay for all of this out of their own budgets.

A friend of mine, John Jackson, is the Chief of Police in Greenwood Village, an upscale bedroom community in metro Denver, and home to my favorite steak in Colorado—*ahhh* Del Frisco's Double Eagle Steak House, you are a special place. Chief Jackson and I were talking the other day and I asked him if he could give me an anonymous quote for this chapter because so many of the other people I knew weren't into going on the record on this subject—kind of politically charged. After giving permission to quote him directly, Chief Jackson got a call and put me on hold while he was informed that no one could be found to prosecute a huge bust they had just made of an illegal grow in a residential neighborhood. All the time-consuming and painstaking work their team had done was down the drain because people are afraid to lose cases and take on The Lobby that seems to get involved in every case they see, so nobody wants to prosecute.

Anyway, I asked Chief Jackson if things had gotten easier or harder for his department since A64 passed. He told me this: "Marijuana is occupying so much of our time. It is freaking out our neighborhoods and filling up our property rooms. We are absolutely *not* getting time back, it's a farce to say that we get more time back than we spend."

We're wasting the cops' time and making their jobs of protecting us harder. We are also giving a very scary message to people who don't like law enforcement. When the U.S. Department of Justice, under former Attorney General Eric Holder, adopted a policy of being selective in enforcing some drug laws and not others, as is the case with the federal marijuana policy, it was essentially saying: "If you don't like a law, screw it, don't pay attention to it." When you see police talking about how good legalization is or would be they are typically retired and are on the LEAP (Law Enforcement Against Prohibition) payroll, in other words, they are getting paid to say that stuff. Ask the cops actually on the ground in states with commercial THC what they think.

I promised a soapbox message so here it is: DON'T GET SO HIGH AMERICA! Consider that the drugs you are doing really do harm to someone other than yourself and your loved ones. They contribute to violent cartels hell-bent on making quick and easy money any way they can. If that means kidnapping and torture, okay. If it means dumping meth into our communities, well all right, they don't care. They want to drive gold-plated Hummers and will stop at nothing to keep that money pouring in. And sad as it is we will wait in line to give it to them.

What if we became a country that consumed very little in the way intoxicating substances? Right now, according to the American Public Health Association, we have 5 percent of the world's population and consume two-thirds of the world's drugs. If we were a place where "rites of passage" in college were things like learning to change a tire or do your own laundry rather than sitting in a dorm and dodging the RA's while we got high. Where freedom of choice didn't mean driving under the influence, and were so marginalized and unaccepted by our society that only the hardened addicts would dream of getting behind the wheel stoned. I love the idea that we might someday become a people who are so proud of our collective success and well-being that we spend our time and energy figuring out how to eradicate global warming or poverty. Where we could focus on protecting and caring for our disenfranchised and marginalized neighbors more than getting them to buy dope. A place where we no longer needed a dozen rehabs in each town. Nothing would make me happier than to work myself out of a job because in addition to there being less pain and suffering in the world, there would be less of a market for the cartels to exploit.

CHAPTER 10

Medical Marijuana

Way More Complex Than Either Side Is Telling You

This is the chapter I have avoided writing, it's going to be painful. I have friends, we all have friends, who suffer and for whom marijuana seems to help. I don't intend to criticize those people. Whatever respect I have maintained or earned thus far from those who sit on one side of this conversation I am likely to lose herein, and I'm bummed about that. I thought a great deal about omitting this whole chapter from the book but it is just too important to skip.

I might as well get right to it, I'm going to make a bunch of statements that are all true but many seem to contradict themselves; that's why this issue is so complex.

✓ Marijuana is a very interesting plant with real medicinal qualities.
  I have friends who have benefitted from consuming marijuana in a
  medicinal manner.
✓ You don't smoke medicine.
✓ Consuming marijuana has improved many lives.
✓ Consuming marijuana has ruined many lives.
✓ Some people suffering from different ailments can find relief
  with marijuana.
✓ Marijuana isn't a miracle plant that cures everything.
✓ Medicine isn't produced or validated by public vote.
✓ There are components within cannabis that might have the ability to
  really improve life for some people.

Evidence that marijuana does what many claim it does for a variety of ailments has yet to withstand rigorous study. Medicines are proven effective when they undergo double-blind testing and placebo controlled experiments.

We must consider the downsides as well as the upsides when considering if we want to call something medicine.

Also consider this: nobody is prescribed marijuana by a doctor. Since it's a Schedule I controlled substance no doctor can prescribe it, even if they wanted to. All a physician can do in states where it is legal is "recommend" a patient use it. Doctors do not prescribe weed, for anything. Just keep that in mind.

Before I get specific let me say this very clearly: If marijuana relieves pain and suffering for the very sick and dying then go for it. No one I know in this conversation would wish suffering on others. For those of you who find relief by using weed, I wish you nothing but the best. If I were you I would be downright pissed that this conversation has devolved into what it is today because you are being exploited more often than not so that people can get high.

Weed does not cure anything. Weed does relieve some painful symptoms and makes some people feel better. Intoxicants do that. Think back to the snake oil of centuries past; it was good for what ailed you no matter what that was because it was mostly hard liquor, intoxicants will do that. To say it will cure a toothache isn't true; however if one is intoxicated enough they won't feel the toothache, so in a way it does help. In a society as pain averse as ours, I have no doubt that weed is helping people feel less physical pain. Going back to the toothache analogy, the tooth hurts because decay has exposed the nerves. You can numb the nerves so you won't feel the pain, but unless you cure the problem by removing the decay, it will hurt again eventually when you aren't drunk or stoned.

We know that the vast majority of people using "medical" marijuana do so for alleged pain. In Colorado, for instance, over 93 percent of the roughly 95,000 people on our medical marijuana registry are on it for pain. To get on the registry, you pay a $35 fee—pretty much anywhere, including at concerts—though you supposedly need to have a serious medical condition and have a doctor send in lots of paperwork. It has been watered down now to a point where it means nothing more than that you paid your fee. As far as pain goes, not only is it subjective, there isn't a test for it other than what patients report. We can't put your blood into a machine and tell you that your pain is a six out of ten, you have to tell the doctor what it is. Given that there isn't a way to test for pain it is an easy thing to exploit, and it is exploited pretty profoundly. Consider these statistics:

✓ In Colorado the total number of medical marijuana cardholders at the time this was written is 94,577
✓ Of those cardholders, 88,209 of them claim "severe pain"
✓ The age group with the highest number of people represented on the entire list is 21 to 30 representing 19,953 of those card holders

While there are certainly exceptions, young people typically aren't suffering from the debilitating conditions that marijuana laws are passed to treat, such as Crohn's disease, ALS, seizures, Parkinson's disease, etc. People in that age demographic and in those numbers are not typically dying of cancer; they like to get high. To anyone in that age group reading this who does have a tragic illness, I wish you the very best and know that I am not talking about you. The reality is that *most* people on our marijuana registry are there because they want to get high, and in Colorado they can get high for less money if they have a med card; it's a tax thing. Medical marijuana is taxed at a much lower rate than is recreational THC.

"Medical marijuana is a red herring to help usher in legalized marijuana." [11] These are not my words; they belong to Keith Stroup, the head of NORML, in an article that appeared in Emory University's *The Emory Wheel* in February 1979. The reality is that for all their talk about helping the sick and dying The Lobby has long used suffering people for their selfish ends: the commercialization of weed. They parade the sick in front of lawmakers, point the cameras at them, and have them tell their genuinely heart-wrenching stories. Then they use those stories as a smokescreen to get paid. It's foul. No lawmaker who wants to be elected again can vote to keep "medicine" away from very

---

11 *The Emory Wheel*, February 6, 1979, pp 18–19.

old or very young people who say it helps them. While these people make up almost every single example given to lawmakers and to the public, cardholders in Colorado, under eleven and over seventy-one, represent less than 4 percent of everyone on the list. When we think of medical marijuana the images that come to mind are babies with seizures, senior citizens with crippling arthritis, and people undergoing harsh chemotherapy treatments.

But in reality, it's a tiny portion of people using marijuana who look like these truly suffering people. Most users are younger than I am and cite a condition that can't be quantified as the reason why they need weed. Stroup was right, it's a hell of a "red herring." For those of you with serious debilitating conditions, they are using you. You are a means to an end for them and that end looks like Colorado. Before A64 passed and we just had medical retail, I watched a young man—who looked to be about nineteen or twenty years old— get out of a car and walk into a medical marijuana dispensary while his three friends waited in the vehicle. A minute later, the door opened and he came out carrying a brown paper bag. He literally jumped off the porch and ran to his buddies in the car. Was he overjoyed because he could solve a serious medical issue? What do you think? This is what much of medical marijuana in this state *really* looks like.

Considerations for
Medical Marijuana Studies

Now that we've covered that part, there is some real evidence that weed helps with some conditions: wasting syndrome associated with AIDS/HIV; muscle spasticity associated with multiple sclerosis (MS); and improving appetite in some patients undergoing chemo. There is also some compelling anecdotal evidence that it might help a very specific type of seizure disorder in young people. This needs further study—and by doctors who care about patients and not selling weed. Not only does the federal government need to get out of the way of that research taking place, they should provide funds to get it done quickly.

Those medical marijuana studies will need to show:

a. It is much more helpful than harmful among the study group;

b. It is better than other treatments used to address the same condition(s);

c. How it interacts with other drugs; and

d. What dosages might look like.

Let's take a quick look at each of these areas.

More good than harm

If someone is using weed to treat a condition but a more serious condition (addiction, psychosis, etc.) can come about as a result of its use, then the bad cancels out the good. The severity of the condition needs to be considered alongside the severity of the side effects. Medicines have side effects, so weed would be no different. To claim otherwise is to use the good in order to ignore the bad. Particular focus should be given to children and adolescents in this category. If we determine that weed reduces acne but increases mental illness then it's not a good acne treatment no matter how many pimples it gets rid of. We also need to be careful using it as a substitute for established medicines. There are young patients at our Children's Hospital in Colorado, for instance, who have very serious medical issues and are taking medicine prescribed by their doctors. If parents decided to pull them off these meds and give them weed or a weed derivative instead, some of the results could be-life threatening.

I spoke with a gentleman last year (family of a dear friend) who called to ask me about weed. He had a brain tumor and was dying. He read an article and wanted to smoke weed to cure the tumor. A report came out a few years ago showing synthesized CBD (about 10,000 times of that found in the plant) reduced the size and growth of some brain tumors. The unfounded message that was delivered was that weed cures brain cancer. I told this man that he needed to talk to his oncologist and not me. He said he was not going back to him because the treatment was awful and he was going to try weed instead. That was a mistake. His doctors knew what they were doing in treating his cancer better than the dude who wrote that article. I told him that if he wanted to smoke weed to go ahead, but certainly don't let kids see and definitely don't drive. But I begged him to make that decision with his doctor, not on his own based on something he read online—that's scary.

Nothing better out there

The FDA has a rule when considering medicine; it's kind of fun to say, "Drug X is less bad than drug Y." Basically, that means there aren't options available that do better or cause less harm. My friend Sarah, a brilliant chemist from Montana who now lives in Colorado, likes to say that she could get some pain relief from chewing hemlock bark but prefers aspirin, it works better. Five hundred years ago, the anti-inflammatory properties in CBD made it a good option to turn cannabis plants into paste and spread it on swelling, maybe even ingest it from time to time. Now that we have ibuprofen, it wouldn't be as good an option. We have some really good drugs out there to treat almost all conditions for which people are using weed, and we know much more about those drugs than we do about weed. The FDA backs up these drugs, making sure they don't contain pesticides, aren't made by a dude in a garage, have dosage descriptions, and all that kind of good stuff. If weed is going to be considered a serious medicine it also needs to pass these tests.

Interactions

This one is gigantic but a little tough to explain in my preferred tone so I'll give you the CliffsNotes. Drugs interact with other drugs in our bodies the same way any chemical interacts with other chemicals in Petri dishes or in test tubes. Bleach is good. Ammonia is good. Bleach and ammonia together, however, are dangerous. Gunpowder, cool. Fire, cool. Gunpowder plus fire equals *BOOM*. Not all drug/drug interactions are bad. Doctors know this stuff and prescribe with those things in mind. Sometimes drugs get more effective when combined. (Milk is good. Oreos are good. Milk and Oreos are awesome!) Some drug combinations are better than the sum of the two in the same way that the result of mixing substances can be better or worse than those substances alone. *Very little is known about how weed, or the components of weed, interact with other prescription and nonprescription drugs—and that is scary.* We need more time to study this issue well before we encourage people to play chemist with their bodies.

Marijuana is contraindicated (a bad idea medically) for some mental health conditions that we know of for sure. Further study needs to be done before we include those conditions on lists of things that weed supposedly "cures" like PTSD and anxiety. If it helps the suffering person sleep better but also increases their risk of psycho-sis or suicide several times over and they are already susceptible to psychosis, then we have a potential big problem.

Dosage

Somebody tell me another "medicine" that we hand out with these directions for the patient, "Take as much as you like, as often as you like, until you get the effect you prefer." Sounds crazy doesn't it?

I got to contribute ideas to New York's medical marijuana law. One requirement in that proposal was central: a doctor had to tell a patient what the recommended dose was, not the other way around. They did a bunch of things right in that law, including a requirement that pharmacists had to be on site at all dispensaries. In addition, no mari-juana that was smoked could be considered medicine and doctors who recommended medicinal weed needed to have real relationships with patients and prescribe a set amount of time for their patient's use. It's not a perfect law but a better law than most.

Moving on with it, consider that much in nature has medicinal qualities. Medicine extracts those qualities and puts them into a safe format and amount to administer. I highly doubt that rigorous sci-entific study will reveal that smoking the whole cannabis plant is the secret. Like a poppy plant, it will have the ability to make medicine but isn't the best form of medicine in and of itself.

Official Positions of Organizations

I miss Chris Farley. There's a great scene in the movie *Tommy Boy*, when Tommy's dad was teaching him the art of the sale. He told the prospective buyer, "I can get a good look at a T-bone by sticking my head up a bull's ass, but I'd rather take a butcher's word for it." (If you've never seen the movie, I highly recommend it.)

For our purposes, "the butchers" are the professional organizations who spend their time researching and thinking about things like medicines, mental health, and other illnesses. These are the groups whose collective knowledge far surpasses anything we will ever acquire on our own. We should pay careful attention and listen to the professionals who have expended considerable time and resources to seriously explore the issues surrounding medical marijuana. Rather than capture their entire statements, which would get boring, here's a partial list of organizations that officially oppose marijuana as medicine:

American Medical Association
American Academy of Pediatrics
American Society of Addiction Medicine
American Cancer Society
American Psychological Association
American Glaucoma Foundation
National Institute of Drug Abuse
Substance Abuse and Mental Health Services Administration

Consider the likelihood of a nineteen-year-old "budtender" selling weed at the local medical marijuana shop actually knowing more than the American Medical Association. Not likely, right?

Real research into the medical qualities in cannabis is happening, not just in America but around the world. That is a good thing and here's why. Suppose weed is the miracle substance we are told it is and can cure everything from athlete's foot to cancer, that would be awesome! We'd put it in a pill and start passing it out but only *after* it stood up to rigorous testing. Not only am I in full support of continuing and even stepping up research, so are most of the organizations I work with who would be described as "anti" weed.

Sometimes, it seems to me like the only people who *don't* want that kind of actual research are the people selling it at dispensaries and lobbying for its legalization. Our old friend Russ Belville wrote an article about the problem with CBD-only legislation, in which he says "[CBD-only laws] provide a rhetorical shield against the most powerful attack we have against marijuana prohibition, the suffering of patients who use cannabinoid medicines." They want it to continue to be used for everything under the sun with no considerations toward potential harm or side effects. Their reality is that twenty-one to thirty-year-olds smoke a lot of weed and are therefore good customers. "Chronic pain" pays them well.

Until all of the research is done, we will have to settle for the pharma produced, quality controlled, and dose specific options that are out there, such as Sativex and Marinol. Whole books have been written about them and their failure to gain any traction in the market, so I don't want to get into all of that. Bottom line: there are real medicines derived from cannabis or made almost entirely of cannabis but very few people seem to be using them. On the other hand, the media and lots of people everywhere are talking about and expanding new uses daily for weed.

CBD and Charlotte's Web

Cannabis contains **at least sixty** known chemicals called cannabinoids, which activate cannabinoid receptors in the body. As we've discussed throughout this book, tetrahydrocannabinol, THC, is what gets you high. Cannabidiol, or CBD, is where the most interesting potential medicinal benefits are found in weed; a bit oversimplified but the statement works. Not only does CBD *not* get one high, as mentioned before, it actually counteracts the high delivered in THC, pretty cool, right?

Since I don't know all of the specifics here I hate to weigh in but this one is brought up everywhere by people arguing for "medical" marijuana.

A couple of years ago CNN's Dr. Sanjay Gupta fell in love with weed, kind of. In a CNN documentary called *Weed,* he presented the case of the Figi family in Colorado, who had a darling young girl named Charlotte. When she was an infant, Charlotte was diagnosed with a disorder called Dravet's syndrome, a very rare type of childhood epilepsy. She was severely disabled—unable to walk, talk, or eat—and had almost constant seizures. It was very hard stuff to watch, even on tape. In an act of desperation, her family tried treating her with a derivative of weed that was mostly CBD in oil form that she ingested several times a day, and it seemed to really help her seizures. Gupta went all in and the popular takeaway became, "Weed cures seizures." A more accurate one would have been "non-intoxicating oil derived from cannabis plant shows promise in the treatment of rare seizure disorder."

As a parent, I sympathized with the family. If I were in their shoes, I would do anything to help my child in the same way that they did, and what a beautiful thing that she appears to be having fewer seizures. On the other hand, a nation or state can't change its laws because of one case. Nobody ever would arrest her, her parents, or the people making the serum, nobody. This case presents more argument for study but unfortunately none for legalizing "medical" marijuana. We often hear how parents and children are flocking to Colorado to get this serum now renamed "Charlotte's Web"—after Charlotte Figi mentioned above—to treat their loved ones' seizures. Some media reports have made it sound like a modern-day migration with people selling everything they own just to get to the Promised Land. There are 191 children age ten or younger on the Colorado Medical Marijuana Registry with seizure disorders. *This is a rare illness and not something that typically gets this kind of attention, unless of course somebody (the Industry) wants to use the kids as red herrings to get paid.*

I am hardly scratching the surface of this issue but I am not the guy to go further with it. Much has been written and much more will be as we continue to learn. I believe the evidence shows that we can make real medicine out of cannabis and that there are yet-to-be-discovered/proven medical uses. I also believe the way medical marijuana is playing out in this country is a joke being told by the people who want to profit from selling it. Sick people are being exploited and real research isn't being demanded because twenty-year-olds want to get high more than society and big pharma wants research to find medicines for people like Charlotte. There's not much money to be made in that.

Consider this "evidence" of the true state of medical marijuana. Real pharmacies don't have "patient drives" and a person who only prescribes one kind of medicine is a pusher, not a doctor.

"Generation Health"—some of you are laughing but the kids
are buying it (literally and figuratively).

Note that it isn't $45 for an evaluation; it's $45 for an approval!

The Budtender of the Month does look hipper than my real doctor, but would you want him giving you or someone you care about medical advice?

I agree, don't gamble with your medicine, get it from a pharmacy.

Does your pharmacy run Black Friday deals?

While it might be nice, since when do real doctors offer
raffle drawings with cash prizes and daily specials?

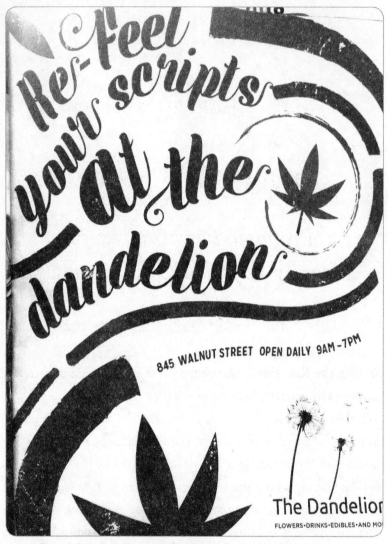

Remember, there is no such thing as "prescribed" marijuana—
but using the language will help people think otherwise.

CHAPTER 11

In a Perfect World

Proposed Laws and Their Insanity Versus Rational Changes

So let's say that this is the direction that we decide we want to move in our country. Let's say we decide to decriminalize or even commercialize THC. Can it be done better? Yes, it can—if it *really is* more important to us to allow for another vice substance to be consumed and "regulated," in a way similar to alcohol. However, this is not the best argument given the many dangerous problems alcohol causes. Still, we could do so much better than the model we have in Colorado. Personally, I would like to see our collective energy focused on combating real local and global issues such as poverty, discrimination, education, clean air and water, terrorism, etc. If we would rather spend our time and treasure figuring out how to get wasted, I submit that this could be done in a more thoughtful way.

Get the corporations out of the equation. Since one can pretty easily grow enough weed to keep one stoned 24/7, why not just let people grow but not allow for retail? If that seems like too much work, how about nonprofit co-ops where people can grow but not make money above the bare essentials required to grow to exchange with others? Why not put a few barriers between people who want to get high and their ability to get high, and make them garden a little bit? There would be no major environmental issues with people growing their own, no advertising campaigns encouraging people to "smoke weed every day," no lobbyists, no commercial interests, no investors or celebrity endorsements, no need to capture new users or convert current users to more frequent users. Basically little incentive other than getting high would be the main factor in this scenario.

Implement an ascending penalty structure for lawbreakers. The next component of a more thoughtful approach would be an ascending penalty structure to keep people from operating outside of the law. As it stands now, the legalization laws people are voting on all have strict limits built into them about how high a fine can go (thanks to Uncle DPA), making it less than a slap on the wrist for the people breaking the laws we do have.

Penalties should start off with something small, and then grow those fines and other deterrents pretty seriously with each offense. If it was going to cost someone significant amounts of money to break the laws, they would be less likely to ignore them. The people who consistently break the laws are either bad actors who won't stop selling drugs or users who need help because they are addicted. The treatment court system in this country is a powerful movement that could be used to help repeat user offenders to get sober, as opposed to only punitive measures. Stiff financial penalties for the corporations can encourage adherence to laws but if the writing of laws is always left to The Lobby and The Industry you can bet there won't be much in the way of deterrents built into them; that would be bad for business.

There are a million miles between where this country has traditionally stood on weed and where we are in Colorado. A commercial market with little in the way of deterrents isn't anything like the sensible reform people are being sold. It's kind of like saying, "Texas is too hot for me. I think I'll move to Antarctica." There is plenty of land between the two places. As more states consider legalization we need to consider this: *If we keep letting The Lobby write the laws, we will continue to have a "fox guarding the hen house" situation.* It profits them to have a large and unregulated commercial industry so they will keep proposing laws that allow this.

Anyone really interested in responsible change should look to what New York did to allow for "medicinal" marijuana. It takes real involvement from a physician, one willing to recommend dosage and frequency. Those laws totally restrict smoking anything and require shops to have actual pharmacists onsite to give out the products. There are practical, better ways to do this if we determine to go in that direction.

The Need for Sound Infrastructure and Data Collection

So let's say we do decide to focus our collective energy on this thing (remember I think it's a poor use of time and money, and foolish). What would we need to do?

First off, real data—on health, crime, and driving under the influence—needs to be collected prior to and after legalization/

commercialization in a consistent manner. We need to establish benchmarks of acceptability, with consequences triggered if the results are not acceptable. If we don't set up acceptable numbers prior to changing our laws, The Industry will keep moving the goalposts back, telling us that it isn't that big of a deal, that it's not a trend, just an outlier, or whatever. They continue to do it in Colorado despite now having the highest marijuana use rate (adults and teens) in the country, and the most potent weed on the planet. In the early findings report released by the state in March 2016, the first couple of pages are basically dedicated to explaining why collecting data is really dang hard for them. Page one of the executive summary includes this dandy statement: "Consequently, it is too early to draw any concise conclusions about the potential effects of marijuana legalization or commercialization . . . *and this may always be difficult due to the lack of historical data.*" (Emphasis added.) Without gathering data beforehand you might see broad trends, but the door is left open for The Lobby to add their spin and avoid detection or consequences.

Requiring politicians to set specific thresholds, numbers that will signal when things have gotten bad enough to require intervention, will make it really hard to keep this conversation so one-sided. If we are going to consider the advantages, we need to consider the disadvantages as well. For example, let's say it is agreed upon that a rise in youth use above 2 percent or adult use over 10 percent would be a big deal. In order to see and address this situation two things need to happen:

1. Several years of baseline data need be collected to make sure we have a starting point prior to the introduction of commercialized THC.
2. After commercialization or legalization, the data needs to be gathered in a totally consistent way for a specified amount of time. If the data

reveals gains that exceed predetermined levels, automatic sanctions
need to kick in that could not be interrupted by political tomfoolery (not
the first word that came to my mind, but I'm hoping cleaner language
will encourage lawmakers to take these ideas to heart).

Now that the data problem has been identified, very careful
thought should be given to how it will be gathered and how that
function will remain apolitical. While possible, it would be a challenge. Funding would be the easiest part of the whole deal. All the
tax money we keep hearing about would cover very solid data collection and presentation. Those who profit pay. Funding the initial data
collection, before the advent of new tax revenues, would be a bigger
challenge but could still be accomplished. *Right now we are pretty
much giving a thumbs up to whatever bill the DPA spoon-feeds us. Let's
stop doing that!* Make the implementation of any retail marijuana
be post-dated. In other words, require in the proposed retail law an
explanation of where the money will come from to gather baseline
data. I get that this is a big responsibility but so is changing the entire
course of drug policy in our country. Maybe we could slow up a minute and try to do it wisely. The only people who don't like the idea of
doing this at a slower and wiser pace is The Lobby and The Industry
because it will delay their profits. Public health should always be the
top priority, not an industry's profits.

Onto the infrastructure part. The details of Colorado's Amendment 64 are pretty insane, especially when it comes to the unreason-
able time provisions. For example, section 5 of A64 required that the
state had to determine how to implement many of the details of the
new law before July 1, 2013. Since A64 passed in November 2012,
the state had about eight months to comply. My experience is that it

would take most state governments eight months to officially decide what month comes after January. I'm making a portion of those regulations contained within A64 available below. It's small because I don't want to take up the room, but if you feel like reading it all just look at section 5 of Colorado's Amendment 64, it's public record obviously. This stuff gets much more complicated when you start to think about details such as these.

21 (5) Regulation of marijuana.

22 (a) NOT LATER THAN JULY 1, 2013, THE DEPARTMENT SHALL ADOPT 23 REGULATIONS NECESSARY FOR IMPLEMENTATION OF THIS SECTION. SUCH 24 REGULATIONS SHALL NOT PROHIBIT THE OPERATION OF MARIJUANA 25 ESTABLISHMENTS, EITHER EXPRESSLY OR THROUGH REGULATIONS THAT MAKE 26 THEIR OPERATION UNREASONABLY IMPRACTICABLE. SUCH REGULATIONS SHALL 27 INCLUDE:28 (I) PROCEDURES FOR THE ISSUANCE, RENEWAL, SUSPENSION, AND 29 REVOCATION OF A LICENSE TO OPERATE A MARIJUANA ESTABLISHMENT, WITH 30 SUCH PROCEDURES SUBJECT TO ALL REQUIREMENTS OF ARTICLE 4 OF TITLE 24 OF 31 THE COLORADO ADMINISTRATIVE PROCEDURE ACT OR ANY SUCCESSOR 32 PROVISION;33 (II) A SCHEDULE OF APPLICATION, LICENSING AND RENEWAL FEES, 34 PROVIDED, APPLICATION FEES SHALL NOT EXCEED FIVE THOUSAND DOLLARS, WITH 35 THIS UPPER LIMIT ADJUSTED ANNUALLY FOR INFLATION, UNLESS THE DEPARTMENT1 DETERMINES A GREATER FEE IS NECESSARY TO CARRY OUT ITS RESPONSIBILITIES 2 UNDER THIS SECTION, AND PROVIDED FURTHER, AN ENTITY THAT IS LICENSED 3 UNDER THE COLORADO MEDICAL MARIJUANA CODE TO CULTIVATE OR SELL 4 MARIJUANA OR TO MANUFACTURE MARIJUANA PRODUCTS AT THE TIME THIS 5 SECTION TAKES EFFECT AND THAT CHOOSES TO APPLY FOR A SEPARATE 6 MARIJUANA ESTABLISHMENT LICENSE SHALL NOT BE REQUIRED TO PAY AN 7 APPLICATION FEE GREATER THAN FIVE HUNDRED DOLLARS TO APPLY FOR A 8 LICENSE TO OPERATE A MARIJUANA ESTABLISHMENT IN ACCORDANCE WITH THE 9 PROVISIONS OF THIS SECTION;10 (III) QUALIFICATIONS FOR LICENSURE THAT ARE DIRECTLY AND 11 DEMONSTRABLY RELATED TO THE OPERATION OF A MARIJUANA ESTABLISHMENT;12 (IV) SECURITY REQUIREMENTS FOR MARIJUANA ESTABLISHMENTS;13 (V) REQUIREMENTS TO PREVENT THE SALE OR DIVERSION OF MARIJUANA 14 AND MARIJUANA PRODUCTS TO PERSONS UNDER THE AGE OF TWENTY-ONE;15 (VI) LABELING REQUIREMENTS FOR MARIJUANA AND MARIJUANA 16 PRODUCTS SOLD OR DISTRIBUTED BY A MARIJUANA ESTABLISHMENT;17 (VII) HEALTH AND SAFETY REGULATIONS AND STANDARDS FOR THE 18 MANUFACTURE OF MARIJUANA PRODUCTS AND THE CULTIVATION OF MARIJUANA;19 (VIII) RESTRICTIONS ON THE ADVERTISING AND DISPLAY OF MARIJUANA 20 AND MARIJUANA PRODUCTS; AND 21 (IX) CIVIL PENALTIES FOR THE FAILURE TO COMPLY WITH REGULATIONS 22 MADE PURSUANT TO THIS SECTION.23 (b) IN ORDER TO ENSURE THE MOST SECURE, RELIABLE, AND ACCOUNTABLE 24 SYSTEM FOR THE PRODUCTION AND DISTRIBUTION OF MARIJUANA AND MARIJUANA 25 PRODUCTS IN ACCORDANCE WITH THIS SUBSECTION, IN ANY COMPETITIVE 26 APPLICATION PROCESS THE DEPARTMENT SHALL HAVE AS A PRIMARY 27 CONSIDERATION WHETHER AN APPLICANT:28 (I) HAS PRIOR EXPERIENCE PRODUCING OR DISTRIBUTING MARIJUANA OR 29 MARIJUANA PRODUCTS PURSUANT TO SECTION 14 OF THIS ARTICLE AND THE 30 COLORADO MEDICAL MARIJUANA CODE IN THE LOCALITY IN WHICH THE 31 APPLICANT SEEKS TO OPERATE A MARIJUANA ESTABLISHMENT; AND1 (II) HAS, DURING THE EXPERIENCE DESCRIBED IN SUBPARAGRAPH (I), 2 COMPLIED CONSISTANTLY WITH SECTION 14 OF THIS ARTICLE, THE PROVISIONS OF 3 THE COLORADO MEDICAL MARIJUANA CODE AND CONFORMING REGULATIONS.4 (c) IN ORDER TO ENSURE THAT INDIVIDUAL PRIVACY IS PROTECTED, 5 NOTWITHSTANDING PARAGRAPH (a), THE DEPARTMENT SHALL NOT REQUIRE A 6 CONSUMER TO PROVIDE A RETAIL MARIJUANA STORE WITH PERSONAL 7 INFORMATION OTHER THAN GOVERNMENT-ISSUED IDENTIFICATION TO DETERMINE 8 THE CONSUMER'S AGE, AND A RETAIL MARIJUANA STORE SHALL NOT BE REQUIRED 9 TO ACQUIRE AND RECORD PERSONAL INFORMATION ABOUT CONSUMERS OTHER 10 THAN INFORMATION TYPICALLY ACQUIRED IN A FINANCIAL TRANSACTION 11 CONDUCTED AT A RETAIL LIQUOR STORE.12 (d) THE GENERAL ASSEMBLY SHALL ENACT AN EXCISE TAX TO BE LEVIED 13 UPON MARIJUANA SOLD OR OTHERWISE TRANSFERRED BY A MARIJUANA 14 CULTIVATION FACILITY TO A MARIJUANA PRODUCT MANUFACTURING FACILITY OR 15 TO A RETAIL MARIJUANA STORE AT A RATE NOT TO EXCEED FIFTEEN PERCENT 16 PRIOR TO JANUARY 1, 2017 AND AT A

RATE TO BE DETERMINED BY THE GENERAL 17 ASSEMBLY THEREAFTER, AND SHALL DIRECT THE DEPARTMENT TO ESTABLISH 18 PROCEDURES FOR THE COLLECTION OF ALL TAXES LEVIED. PROVIDED, THE FIRST 19 FORTY MILLION DOLLARS IN REVENUE RAISED ANNUALLY FROM ANY SUCH EXCISE 20 TAX SHALL BE CREDITED TO THE PUBLIC SCHOOL CAPITAL CONSTRUCTION 21 ASSISTANCE FUND CREATED BY ARTICLE 43.7 OF TITLE 22, C.R.S., OR ANY 22 SUCCESSOR FUND DEDICATED TO A SIMILAR PURPOSE. PROVIDED FURTHER, NO 23 SUCH EXCISE TAX SHALL BE LEVIED UPON MARIJUANA INTENDED FOR SALE AT 24 MEDICAL MARIJUANA CENTERS PURSUANT TO SECTION 14 OF THIS ARTICLE AND 25 THE COLORADO MEDICAL MARIJUANA CODE.26 (e) NOT LATER THAN OCTOBER 1, 2013, EACH LOCALITY SHALL ENACT AN 27 ORDINANCE OR REGULATION SPECIFYING THE ENTITY WITHIN THE LOCALITY THAT 28 IS RESPONSIBLE FOR PROCESSING APPLICATIONS SUBMITTED FOR A LICENSE TO 29 OPERATE A MARIJUANA ESTABLISHMENT WITHIN THE BOUNDARIES OF THE 30 LOCALITY AND FOR THE ISSUANCE OF SUCH LICENSES SHOULD THE ISSUANCE BY 31 THE LOCALITY BECOME NECESSARY BECAUSE OF A FAILURE BY THE DEPARTMENT 32 TO ADOPT REGULATIONS PURSUANT TO PARAGRAPH (a) OR BECAUSE OF A FAILURE 33 BY THE DEPARTMENT TO PROCESS AND ISSUE LICENSES AS REQUIRED BY 34 PARAGRAPH (g).35 (f) A LOCALITY MAY ENACT ORDINANCES OR REGULATIONS, NOT IN 36 CON-FLICT WITH THIS SECTION OR WITH REGULATIONS OR LEGISLATION ENACTED 37 PURSUANT TO THIS SECTION, GOVERNING THE TIME, PLACE, MANNER AND NUMBER81 OF MARIJUANA ESTABLISHMENT OPERATIONS; ESTABLISHING PROCEDURES FOR THE 2 ISSUANCE, SUSPENSION, AND REVOCATION OF A LICENSE ISSUED BY THE LOCALITY 3 IN ACCORDANCE WITH PARAGRAPH (h) OR (i), SUCH PROCEDURES TO BE SUBJECT 4 TO ALL REQUIREMENTS OF ARTICLE 4 OF TITLE 24 OF THE COLORADO 5 ADMINISTRATIVE PROCEDURE ACT OR ANY SUCCESSOR PROVISION; ESTABLISHING 6 A SCHEDULE OF ANNUAL OPERATING, LICENSING, AND APPLICATION FEES FOR 7 MARIJUANA ESTABLISHMENTS, PROVIDED, THE APPLICATION FEE SHALL ONLY BE 8 DUE IF AN APPLI-CATION IS SUBMITTED TO A LOCALITY IN ACCORDANCE WITH 9 PARAGRAPH (i) AND A LICENSING FEE SHALL ONLY BE DUE IF A LICENSE IS ISSUED 10 BY A LOCALITY IN ACCORDANCE WITH PARAGRAPH (h) OR (i); AND ESTABLISHING 11 CIVIL PENALTIES FOR VIOLATION OF AN ORDINANCE OR REGULATION GOVERNING 12 THE TIME, PLACE, AND MANNER OF A MARIJUANA ESTABLISHMENT THAT MAY 13 OPERATE IN SUCH LOCALITY. A LOCALITY MAY PROHIBIT THE OPERATION OF 14 MARIJUANA CULTIVATION FACILITIES, MARIJUANA PRODUCT MANUFACTURING 15 FACILITIES, MARIJUANA TESTING FACILITIES, OR RETAIL MARIJUANA STORES 16 THROUGH THE ENACTMENT OF AN ORDINANCE OR THROUGH AN INITIATED OR 17 REFERRED MEASURE; PROVIDED, ANY INITIATED OR REFERRED MEASURE TO 18 PROHIBIT THE OPERATION OF MARIJUANA CULTIVATION FACILITIES, MARIJUANA 19 PRODUCT MANUFACTURING FACILITIES, MARIJUANA TESTING FACILITIES, OR 20 RETAIL MARIJUANA STORES MUST APPEAR ON A GENERAL ELECTION BALLOT 21 DURING AN EVEN NUMBERED YEAR.22 (g) EACH APPLICATION FOR AN ANNUAL LICENSE TO OPERATE A 23 MARIJUANA ESTABLISHMENT SHALL BE SUBMITTED TO THE DEPARTMENT. THE 24 DEPARTMENT SHALL:25 (I) BEGIN ACCEPTING AND PROCESSING APPLICATIONS ON OCTOBER 1, 2013; 26 (II) IMMEDIATELY FORWARD A COPY OF EACH APPLICATION AND HALF OF 27 THE LICENSE APPLICATION FEE TO THE LOCALITY IN WHICH THE APPLICANT DESIRES 28 TO OPERATE THE MARIJUANA ESTABLISHMENT;29 (III) ISSUE AN ANNUAL LICENSE TO THE APPLICANT BETWEEN FORTY-FIVE 30 AND NINETY DAYS AFTER RECEIPT OF AN APPLICATION UNLESS THE DEPARTMENT 31 FINDS THE APPLICANT IS NOT IN COMPLIANCE WITH REGULATIONS ENACTED 32 PURSUANT TO PARAGRAPH (a) OR THE DEPARTMENT IS NOTIFIED BY THE RELEVANT 33 LOCALITY THAT THE APPLICANT IS NOT IN COMPLIANCE WITH ORDINANCES AND 34 REGULATIONS MADE PURSUANT TO PARAGRAPH (f) AND IN EFFECT AT THE TIME OF 35 APPLICATION, PROVIDED, WHERE A LOCALITY HAS ENACTED A NUMERICAL LIMIT 36 ON THE NUMBER OF MARIJUANA ESTABLISHMENTS AND A GREATER NUMBER OF 37 APPLICANTS SEEK LICENSES, THE DEPARTMENT SHALL SOLICIT AND CONSIDER1 INPUT FROM THE LOCALITY AS TO THE LOCALITY'S PREFERENCE OR PREFERENCES 2 FOR LICENSURE; AND3 (IV) UPON DENIAL OF AN APPLICATION, NOTIFY THE APPLICANT IN WRITING 4 OF THE SPECIFIC REASON FOR ITS DENIAL.5 (h) IF THE DEPARTMENT DOES NOT ISSUE A LICENSE TO AN APPLICANT 6 WITHIN NINETY DAYS OF RECEIPT OF THE APPLICATION FILED IN ACCORDANCE WITH 7 PARAGRAPH (g) AND DOES NOT NOTIFY THE APPLICANT OF THE SPECIFIC REASON 8 FOR ITS DENIAL, IN WRITING AND WITHIN SUCH TIME PERIOD, OR IF THE 9 DEPARTMENT HAS ADOPTED REGULATIONS PURSUANT TO PARAGRAPH (a) AND HAS 10 ACCEPTED APPLICATIONS PURSUANT TO PARAGRAPH (g) BUT HAS NOT ISSUED ANY 11 LICENSES BY JANUARY 1, 2014, THE APPLICANT MAY RESUBMIT ITS APPLICATION 12 DIRECTLY TO THE LOCALITY, PURSUANT TO PARAGRAPH (e), AND THE LOCALITY 13 MAY ISSUE AN ANNUAL LICENSE TO THE APPLICANT. A LOCALITY ISSUING A 14 LICENSE TO AN APPLICANT SHALL DO SO WITHIN NINETY DAYS OF RECEIPT OF THE 15 RESUBMITTED APPLICATION UNLESS THE LOCALITY FINDS AND NOTIFIES THE 16 APPLICANT THAT THE APPLICANT IS NOT IN COMPLIANCE WITH ORDINANCES AND 17 REGULATIONS MADE PURSUANT TO PARAGRAPH (f) IN EFFECT AT THE TIME THE 18 APPLICATION IS RESUBMITTED AND THE LOCALITY SHALL NOTIFY THE DEPARTMENT 19 IF AN ANNUAL LICENSE HAS BEEN ISSUED TO THE APPLICANT. IF AN APPLICATION 20 IS SUBMITTED TO A LOCALITY UNDER THIS PARAGRAPH, THE DEPARTMENT SHALL 21 FORWARD TO THE LOCALITY THE APPLICATION FEE PAID BY

THE APPLICANT TO THE 22 DEPARTMENT UPON REQUEST BY THE LOCALITY. A LICENSE ISSUED BY A LOCALITY 23 IN ACCORDANCE WITH THIS PARAGRAPH SHALL HAVE THE SAME FORCE AND EFFECT 24 AS A LICENSE ISSUED BY THE DEPARTMENT IN ACCORDANCE WITH PARAGRAPH (g) 25 AND THE HOLDER OF SUCH LICENSE SHALL NOT BE SUBJECT TO REGULATION OR 26 ENFORCEMENT BY THE DEPARTMENT DURING THE TERM OF THAT LICENSE. 27 A SUBSEQUENT OR RENEWED LICENSE MAY BE ISSUED UNDER THIS PARAGRAPH ON 28 AN ANNUAL BASIS ONLY UPON RESUBMISSION TO THE LOCALITY OF A NEW 29 APPLICATION SUBMITTED TO THE DEPARTMENT PURSUANT TO PARAGRAPH (g). 30 NOTHING IN THIS PARAGRAPH SHALL LIMIT SUCH RELIEF AS MAY BE AVAILABLE TO 31 AN AGGRIEVED PARTY UNDER SECTION 24-4-104, C.R.S., OF THE COLORADO 32 ADMINISTRATIVE PROCEDURE ACT OR ANY SUCCESSOR PROVISION.33 (i) IF THE DEPARTMENT DOES NOT ADOPT REGULATIONS REQUIRED BY 34 PARAGRAPH (a), AN APPLICANT MAY SUBMIT AN APPLICATION DIRECTLY TO A 35 LOCALITY AFTER OCTOBER 1, 2013 AND THE LOCALITY MAY ISSUE AN ANNUAL 36 LICENSE TO THE APPLICANT. A LOCALITY ISSUING A LICENSE TO AN APPLICANT 37 SHALL DO SO WITHIN NINETY DAYS OF RECEIPT OF THE APPLICATION UNLESS IT 38 FINDS AND NOTIFIES THE APPLICANT THAT THE APPLICANT IS NOT IN COMPLIANCE101 WITH ORDINANCES AND REGULATIONS MADE PURSUANT TO PARAGRAPH (f) IN 2 EFFECT AT THE TIME OF APPLICATION AND SHALL NOTIFY THE DEPARTMENT IF AN 3 ANNUAL LICENSE HAS BEEN ISSUED TO THE APPLICANT. A LICENSE ISSUED BY A 4 LOCALITY IN ACCORDANCE WITH THIS PARAGRAPH SHALL HAVE THE SAME FORCE 5 AND EFFECT AS A LICENSE ISSUED BY THE DEPARTMENT IN ACCORDANCE WITH 6 PARAGRAPH (g) AND THE HOLDER OF SUCH LICENSE SHALL NOT BE SUBJECT TO 7 REGULATION OR ENFORCEMENT BY THE DEPARTMENT DURING THE TERM OF THAT 8 LICENSE. A SUBSEQUENT OR RENEWED LICENSE MAY BE ISSUED UNDER THIS 9 PARAGRAPH ON AN ANNUAL BASIS IF THE DEPARTMENT HAS NOT ADOPTED 10 REGULATIONS REQUIRED BY PARAGRAPH (a) AT LEAST NINETY DAYS PRIOR TO THE 11 DATE UPON WHICH SUCH SUBSEQUENT OR RENEWED LICENSE WOULD BE EFFECTIVE 12 OR IF THE DEPARTMENT HAS ADOPTED REGULATIONS PURSUANT TO PARAGRAPH 13 (a) BUT HAS NOT, AT LEAST NINETY DAYS AFTER THE ADOPTION OF SUCH 14 REGULATIONS, ISSUED LICENSES PURSUANT TO PARAGRAPH (g).

Building a sound infrastructure for something as huge as rolling out a market for another vice substance on a statewide level is a big job, a *very* big job. The people doing it in Colorado—such as Andrew Freedman, the director of marijuana coordination for the state, and Governor John Hickenlooper—tell any journalist who will listen what a great job they are doing, but I see something very different and much of it is because we rushed the implementation process. Maybe their statements are influenced on wanting to keep their jobs?

Not only is there a ton of detailed law and regulation to pen, there are physical preparations to be made as well. Guidelines for use and retail take time to write and implement and the political machine seems to lack much urgency. We should create committees with stakeholders of varying backgrounds (heavy on public health please) and give them specific responsibilities. In Colorado, most work groups were influenced by industry representatives who ended up sitting on them. We need to seriously consider the ramifications of these very complicated issues in order to find reasonable, safe, sensible solutions, rather than simple answers and "good enough" public policy.

While creating the written infrastructure is much of the heavy lifting required prior to rollout, there are plenty of things to get into place physically. If you have followed this issue at all in Colorado, you know that we are super proud of our "seed to sale" tracking labels on each plant. We require that every plant has a radio transmitter the whole time it is being grown to make sure that no hanky-panky, like growing plants that aren't part of the legal sales system, takes place. Officials loved to talk about it before January 1, 2014, when retail opened, and they still reference it all the time as one of our big successes. With that in mind you might find it surprising to learn that the majority of the hardware for this tracking wasn't even in the state of Colorado on January 1, 2014, let alone during the grow fest that preceded the opening of recreational retail dispensaries. This should be a huge indicator of how hard all of this really is to implement!

A few other problems that will need physical solutions:

- ✓ Proactive training of significantly more drug recognition experts (DREs) to keep stoned drivers accountable until someone invents the THC breathalyzer.
- ✓ Retirement of drug dogs who have been trained to sniff out weed and training a new batch to look only for other illegal substances. (Right now, they detect all substances, including weed, but obviously can't tell officers which one they have found.)
- ✓ HAZMAT readiness to deal with mold at grow sites and BHO explosions
- ✓ Expanded evidence storage capabilities for law enforcement. Illegally trafficked weed needs to be held in evidence, and the quantities are

substantial. Weed takes up lots of space and traffickers will still be
arrested and prosecuted.

✓ Offices, supplies, cars, training, and all that stuff for whatever agency
will be responsible for enforcing laws and regulations. (I've got to throw
this out there to all of my libertarian friends who love limited government
and think this is a way of getting Uncle Sam out of your state; did you
ever consider how many more state employees are required to manage
this process? This isn't limiting government, it's making it bigger.)

The amount of time it will take to get all of these issues ironed out
depends on several factors in each state. When determining what the
lead-in time should be, one would want to consider existing infrastructure (such as the medical enforcement division) and how well
those departments are performing. Just because an enforcement division exists doesn't mean they are necessarily effective or are prepared
for the issues of the scale that will arise when going from medical to
recreational pot.

Colorado had an inept medical marijuana enforcement infrastructure according to a report called "Medical Marijuana Licensing Perfor-
mance Audit," published by the state in July 2013. The audit accused the
health department of not sufficiently overseeing doctors who give out
the recommendations to patients for medical marijuana. In 2009, there
were 6,000 medical marijuana patients in Colorado, but by March 2013,
the list had grown to 108,000 patients. As of 2012, 903 Colorado doctors
recommended medical marijuana "red cards" for those patients, but
only a dozen of those doctors issued half of the recommendations. One
doctor recommended that a patient have over 500 marijuana plants.
Does that sound reasonable for one person? What made people think
that just making that group bigger would make it work better?

States also need to consider their size and the business climate that exists there. A place like California will be infinitely more complex to roll out recreational weed than Oklahoma, even though California already has a huge medical marijuana industry and Oklahoma has neither. California is so much larger and more diverse that it will take a much bigger effort there than it would in a state with one or two metropolitan areas.

Other Areas of Concern

For the record, I still think we should be spending our time on other issues, and I am not advocating that we change laws nationwide to mimic Colorado. Also, for the record, I think that *O Brother, Where Art Thou* is the funniest movie of all time. These things being said, I know that not everybody agrees with me on either point, unfortunately. So again, if we do this, we should be smart about it—and try watching that movie again. It gets better every time and is about as funny as it gets.

Disclaimer done, onto problem solving. There are a bunch of issues that need to be fixed. Here are a few:

Banking

Banks in the United States are insured by the Federal Deposit Insurance Corporation (FDIC). It is an independent agency created by Congress during the Great Depression to maintain stability and public confidence in the nation's financial system. Since the FDIC has to follow federal law, banks that are insured by the FDIC can't knowingly take money that was made illegally, i.e., selling a federally illegal substance. As discussed earlier, marijuana and its derivatives are still considered a Schedule 1 narcotic and are illegal federally. Because of this, dispensaries and other marijuana-related enterprises can't keep their money in banks, so the business in Colorado is all cash—*hundreds of millions of dollars floating around, all in cash.* Colorado has tried a bunch of times to fix this on its own and the Obama administration had even tried another one of its memos (written by Deputy Attorney General James M. Cole), nothing has worked. Banks are risk-averse organizations and they are going to follow the law. We have tried to build collective, co-op style banks, have tried creating weed-only institutions, all sorts of things, to no avail. There is literally around $100 million in cash for THC changing hands around the state most months. You don't need a PhD in criminology to know what happens when there are tons of drugs and huge amounts of cash in one place—lots of robberies. Apparently many of these crimes go unreported, "Um, yeah, I'm calling to report someone stole my weed." However, there are several calls like this every day that come in to local police. Crime in and around dispensaries is a big deal in this all-cash big business.

The other issue is that a cash-rich economy provides way more opportunity for laundering money from other "ventures." Too much cash in an area makes it easier for the bad guys to clean up their dirty money. It also raises some interesting questions about tax collection. Answer truthfully now: if your income were all in cash would you report all of it to the tax man?

To fix this issue it would basically take an act of Congress. To bring the weed industry into mainstream financial markets could be done, but it would be pretty involved and would entail establishing significant safeguards to make sure that this wasn't the easiest way for criminals to wash their money. The effort would have to be led by the FDIC I think and have some pretty high level support on the Hill. Until we fix this one, we need to stop opening stores. Or I guess we could keep hiring more and more "enforcer" guys to guard the cash with automatic weapons. Have you ever been to a developing nation, where there is a big gap between the "haves" and the "have-nots"? The "haves" usually have guys around who look a lot like they are ready for combat.

Smells

Now that we've discussed all the difficult financial stuff, let's solve an easier, more obvious problem: weed has a very distinctive smell that is pretty strong. On a trip to the zoo at the end of the summer last year, my then six-year-old asked if there were skunks in the parking lot. Even at 8:00 AM on a Saturday at a family-friendly place I got to have yet another talk with my kids about drug use.

Last year, a buddy of mine had to move from his super awesome and pretty swanky condo in Denver. Not only was the place right in the heart of everything, he could order "room service" from Elway's steakhouse! It overlooked Coors Field and had amazing mountain views. Unfortunately, his neighbors smoked weed—apparently that is about all they did—and the smell ended up being too much for him and his wife. The shared walls and shared HVAC system made it feel like they were in the same room. Conversations with the neighbors and the management got them nowhere so they moved.

Smoking weed has somehow become a right in Colorado and heaven forbid you tell someone you don't want to smell their weed; they flip out and talk about their constitutional rights.

Fortunately, this one is pretty easy to fix. You can't smoke weed in public in Colorado, but we need to do a better job of enforcing it.

Laws about tobacco need to apply to weed. In my buddy's situation, *were it tobacco, the building would have backed him in a second, because it is established and accepted that he has a right to clean air in his home more than the others have a right to smoke.* Things are backwards in Colorado (thank you Industry lawyers), now the THC smokers have the rights and the rest of us have to live with it.

There are lots of forms of consumption now that do not require smoking. Mandate people use those in places where your neighbors might smell or my kids could be walking by. Eat a gummy bear rolled in sugar, sip 1/35th of a soda, have a cup of weed coffee.

The reality is that there are hundreds of ways to get high on THC today. If this is going to work, the consumers are going to have to consider the rest of us a little bit as we are asked to consider them. The inevitable question asked by consumers, actually asked by The Lobby/Industry on behalf of the consumers, is "Well, where can I smoke?"

My answer to that is, "I don't know, not my issue." Those who choose to consume should be responsible for figuring out how to do so without affecting everyone around them. People still smoke cigarettes and cigars, just less and not in public. Look to the cigarette smokers for an example of how to do things (yeah, I said that).

We also have issues with smells around grow operations and storage. There's a device called a "nasal ranger" and it directs the smeller so he or she can identify where the weed smell is coming from. It kind of looks like a blow dryer that the operator wears on his or her nose. Google it, it looks as strange as it sounds.

We just need to hire more people willing to put these things on their faces and write tickets. Maybe we should require The Industry to provide this device in Colorado because the smell of grow houses and weed stores gets pretty bad. I'm worried far less about how we would pay for all of those people than I am where in the hell we would find enough people willing to put that thing on their face in public. Maybe a *Star Trek* convention or something? Sorry, Mom, and all the other Trekkies out there, you're awesome. You just don't always seem to have the "looking dignified" thing down. Good news though; your country or at least my state, needs you!

I mentioned the need for recycling the air in my truck at a spot on my commute, but you should smell it downtown! There is an odor of weed in Denver that isn't just burning plants; it's from growing and storing them.

Seriously, this one is also easily solved by enforcing existing laws on the smell. The large cultivation facilities need a more high-tech solution, really good air filtration systems. They aren't cheap but hey, that's the cost of doing business!

The First Amendment

Before A64 passed, I was in California, participating in a panel discussion alongside three other people, debating the pros and cons of legalization. One of the people on the other side of the discussion was a woman named Amanda Reiman. At that time, she was in academia and doing some work to change weed laws. Today, she is the director of the California chapter of the DPA. During the debate the topic of advertising came up. I shared my fears that we will not contain the advertisements to responsible stuff (like not having cartoon characters selling weed) unless it's clearly mandated and wondered how we do that while preserving citizens' First Amendment rights. The intersection of American-style capitalism, vice substances, and the marketing of them doesn't exactly have the best track record practically speaking and I saw no reason why this would be any different.

Amanda told me I was wrong and went on to make a case that The Industry would be their own police because they had so much to lose if they advertised recklessly. Well, I'll let you be the judge on this one. Are these examples of responsible advertising geared toward adults who choose to consume responsibly?

A bus with all-you-can-smoke weed—and free drinks.

A teddy bear on a rocket telling a college town to stay high.
That's responsible?

That's an interesting back-to-school special.

"Show us how you make the good times better" translates to
"Send us pics of you getting high and doing stuff."
The stoned snowboarder is pretty funny.
Unless, of course, you or your kids like to ski/ride on the same
mountain as the stoned chick taking pics of the good times.

Okay, you get the point, but I couldn't resist a few more photos; there are just so many to choose from! Two weeks after A64 passed the lawsuits started, the first one was over advertising and weed mags. The Industry won and that victory for free speech was also a sign of things to come. Unless they are required to agree to restrictions in the same way tobacco and hard liquor have been regulated, we're in real trouble.

Here is my proposed solution: we agree to only black-and-white words. No pictures of Santa, cartoons, clip art, half-naked women, candy, etc. Advertising is thereby extremely limited and we don't have to leave it up to the people selling the stuff to police themselves, because they won't—ever.

Limiting Potency

An effort to cap THC content at 16 percent recently failed in the Colorado legislature. The Lobby made a big stink and this rather thoughtful legislation proposed by SMART Colorado was pretty much DOA. It was frustrating to watch it play out. Sixteen percent was recommended as the number because it is the highest THC content that we have any credible research on (remember that study in *The Lancet*). We are discussing the dangers of a plant when it's more of a GMO, and more realistically a synthetic drug that we are dealing with. Limiting potency to reflect the ceiling of scientific research makes really rational sense and should have passed with ease but it didn't.

End of rant, now for the solution: build potency limits into every law that passes. There will, of course, be issues that come up about how to do this practically, but that is okay. If they want to make money selling the stuff it should be done on reasonable terms. While 16 percent THC potency is pretty scary considering mental health, addiction, and brain development issues, at least we have some research on it.

Since commercially produced weed is typically far above 16 percent, our society is effectively telling people that it's okay and The Industry is directly telling them it's okay. This should stop.

Solving the issue would mean labs in the state need to agree on a uniform way to test (actually much harder than you may think) and then the manufacturers/retailers need to submit enough samples to prove that they are in compliance. Sending a sample or two a year isn't enough. It needs to be a true representative sample that is tested, and those samples need to be both predictably regular and randomized. To this The Industry will say that it would be cost-restrictive and take too much time. I answer that with "Okay, if you want to sell it, you need to be responsible for it." If we need to spend more money to make sure we aren't getting miles ahead of the science I'm okay with that. They will also say that it would essentially kill the concentrates industry. I also answer okay to that one. Concentrates are a synthetic drug that don't have a place in society, I'm good with that market going away; less mess for the rest of us to clean up.

It would be simple to make sure that the 16 percent potency requirement is met. Institute progressive fines for violators with real teeth for enforcing them. The first fine should sting and make the offender realize they need to be more careful. And, just like in criminal justice, if violations continue the penalty should increase until it is a poor risk/rewards equation to continue violating the law. Limiting potency reduces harm.

Packaging

Everything that contains THC should come in opaque childproof packaging instead of kid-friendly advertising on easy-to-access packages. This idea is so simple that I won't waste much ink on it. We do it with everything else that can be harmful to children, why not weed? That question was rhetorical; the answer is of course The Lobby.

Driving

Here's a huge public safety issue! Testing someone for THC impairment is complex. At this point it is almost impossible. The science just isn't there, or even close to being there. We can see when somebody recently consumed but THC metabolizes unpredictably, unlike alcohol. Think about the incentive out there for someone to develop a breathalyzer-style test to show impairment; we're talking potentially several billion dollars. Every law enforcement agency in the developed world would buy as many as you could make—and their checks clear! If it were easy to test for impairment somebody would be very, very rich right now. Some of the smart people I know tell me that the issue is so complex that it won't be solved in my lifetime and that makes it a *huge* issue. If we are going to create space for growing numbers of people to get high on THC, then the driving thing needs to be figured out *immediately*. I have a solution for this one as well, but I warn you, if you consume THC you aren't going to like it!

Driving isn't a right, but those who are on the roads (bikes and pedestrians included) do have a right to expect that those around them are not impaired. If a person chooses to consume THC, that choice might have to cost them something very real, in this case, their driving privileges.

Since THC can stay in your system for a long time, over twenty-eight days, obviously not everyone with THC in their bloodstream will be impaired, quite unlike alcohol. With that in mind, I say that the *rights* of people on the roads outweigh the *privilege* of smoking weed. If you have THC in your system you don't get to drive. It's harsh and not at all perfect but it's a solution that puts public safety above intoxication. The legal limits and recommendations about how much THC can be in a driver's system are silly and the numbers were basically assigned by people with little to no understanding of the complex science and chemistry involved. If you want to really understand this complex subject, listen to Courtney Popp, Washington State traffic safety resource prosecutor and legal advisor for the King County Sheriff's Office present sometime. The bottom line is that in Colorado five nanograms—that is, one *billionth* of a gram—of THC per milliliter of blood is considered intoxicated.

There are, however, plenty examples of heavy users not being impaired with a higher THC count in their blood as well as people being tried and convicted of driving under the influence when their level was lower that the legal limit. One such case just played out in my neighborhood. About two miles from my house, twenty-year-old Kyle Couch ran over an eight-year-old girl out for a bike ride with her dad. Despite his car window being down and the father yelling at him to stop, he was too out of it to notice and hit and killed the little girl. He later said, "I thought I ran over a curb." Kyle failed a roadside sobriety test and the drug recognition expert (DRE), a specially trained police officer, cited marijuana intoxication. Although he was clearly intoxicated on THC, stoned enough to mistake a little girl for a curb, his blood only tested at 1.5 ng/ml, way below the set "limit." He is being charged with DUI for marijuana, no other substances.

When someone develops a way to test for roadside impairment from THC I will take this all back, and I hope I get invited out on their boat someday; I'm sure it will be a nice one.

So weed smokers of the world unite! Get Richard Branson (DPA

Board remember) to fund the research and development, and find a way that you can prove to the rest of us who use roads to drive our kids to school on, as well as bike and walk on, that you are sober. Invent a weed breathalyzer device and I will be the first in line to cheer the accomplishment. *With the privilege comes the responsibility.*

Why We Get High

We are hardwired to do things that make us feel better in the moment. I don't have the patience or the credentials to get into the brain science here, but we all know it's true. Drugs make us feel better for a minute. They block out pain and some of them make us feel light and put a smile on our faces. The issue is when we get too used to that feeling and chase it above other more important things. That's why drugs cause harm. Unfortunately, by the time we realize that they are too important we can have a hard time stopping because we have grown so used to this form of pleasure. We keep getting high then because we often forget how, or are not able to, feel good without a substance.

We get high to feel better, to forget, to fit in; all of the things I mentioned a few chapters ago. Some of us even get high to make connecting with others easier, and that connection or perceived connection is a big deal even though it centers around an intoxicant. Some of us have had such a tough go of it that we can't imagine being in a room with other people sober; it's too scary. We crave that connection but don't think we can get it without some chemical aid. People bond over drugs in many ways and use them to feel that bond. In recovery, we say that we need to change people and places; the people part of that can be terrifying.

I remember this fear when I got sober. What would I do? Who would I talk to? How would I connect with others? The reality that my connections were dependent on sharing drugs didn't hit for a while, and when it did the hollowness of that connection was hard to ignore. When we have to form bonds around other things besides drugs, our relationships take on a much more real and risky component. We get to know one another on a level much deeper than a shared affinity for a particular mind-altering substance. While that can be scary at first, it is beautiful and fulfilling once the fear starts to bed down. We get high in the hopes of feeling good and connecting, but *in reality we condition our bodies to feel good only when high and to connect around shallow things that do not, or should not, define who we are as people.*

How We Could Change It All. This Isn't About Weed

I've saved this section, writing it last before shipping this thing out. I anticipated this being the best part to write and have been, as Dr. M. Scott Peck instructs in *The Road Less Traveled*, "delaying the gratification" of writing it.

I'm so damn tired of talking about weed, but this isn't really about weed. I think people deal with pain, hardship, loneliness, disappointment, boredom, stress, fear, anger, etc. in different ways. Mankind has always dealt with these things, to some degree, by numbing with intoxicants. But I can't help but feel like things are changing. It appears to me that we are relying more and more on things that change our mood and get us out of ourselves and distance us from reality. That is what it's really about, I think.

Pain, hardship, anger, etc., are all part of life. They are not fun but oftentimes they are the parts from which we grow the most. This isn't an autobiography so I'm not getting into details, but I know a thing or two about pain. Physical, mental, emotional, long-term, acute, and so on. Pain isn't something to enjoy but it also isn't something to ignore or run away from. Pain can also protect us from more dangerous things. If we put our hand on a hot stove but couldn't feel the pain, we would still get burned and could die from the infection.

Life isn't about masking pain/uncomfortable feelings at all costs; the idea of that kind of vanilla existence scares me. For me, living has been about trying to find a way to integrate those things into who I am and into my daily life. By attempting to live "life on life's terms," I get to be right where I am, which means I need to find ways to work through the things that aren't comfortable in the moment. The beauty in doing this is getting to know oneself and those around us in ways that elude us when we choose to escape into intoxication.

People have always gotten wasted and they always will, no matter the laws. What I am observing are higher numbers of people getting intoxicated to escape; more than I believe have tried at any point in our history. Maybe it's a case of having more access to more intoxicants than ever before. Whatever the causes, my real fear is that if we keep going down this path of accepting intoxication as the norm rather than the exception, fewer people will grow to their fullest, individually and as a society. I have a friend who likes to say that character is more important than comfort. I like that one because in a world where comfort becomes more important than character, what can we expect?

I know I can get a little preachy but I am obviously very impassioned. While I can be brash and crass at times I do not intend anything I've said to be rude or thoughtless. I respect the right that everyone has to make their own decisions and to lead the life that is set before them, within reason, remembering that we are all in this together, to an extent. However, I do not apologize for my words directly opposing The Industry and Lobby. You guys embody what is wrong with America, in my eyes, and I would like to see your energy and intellect put to better uses, for building up rather than tearing down. You have deep resources and much to offer; you can do more than figure out ways for more people to get higher. Just consider that.

To those of you in situations similar to what mine was, I'm cheering and praying for you. Ask for help and don't stop until you get it. You are worth it and there is a rich and full life out there that your most ambitious dreams fall short of. I know this from experience.

CHAPTER 12

The Arguments and the Rebuttals

How to Respond to What the Seventeen-Year-Olds Throw at You

Have you have ever gone toe-to-toe with a teenager about weed? What about one who was raised by suckling the sweet milk of DPA talking points? If you have, what follows should be of particular interest. Not that this subject is just for teenagers to argue. I find that the extreme open-mindedness that exists in some circles of our society has led to these ideas being embraced by the crowd that is open to just about anything other than logic.

The professors and academic elites who love to comment from afar while looking down on the hoi polloi from their ivory towers also get into embracing The Lobby's talking points. These guys are some of my favorite people to debate. While they sit back and tell us how it should all work well, very rarely have their opinions been influenced by real-life experiences. In theory, many ideas should work well, but in reality they don't. These "experts" enjoy the freedom that comes by oversimplifying issues and twisting facts to fit their positions. While I can feel very sorry for the kids I debate with who are just pawns in The Industry's game, the elites should know what they're doing. As such, I have no problem squaring off with them in a debate.

The arguments are predictable and pretty simple. Americans seems to love simplicity when it comes to politics, but they are easily refuted if you are willing to engage. The arguments below have been used to justify a major shift in policy. They rationalize and protect an industry that is laughing all the way to the bank because others are making their points for them while they make all of the money.

As I mentioned in the previous chapter, the Rocky Mountain High Intensity Drug Trafficking Area (HIDTA) report is one of best sources of actual data you will find coming out of Colorado. Because I get into so many of these conversations, I actually carry around a copy of it, full of my notes, just about everywhere I go. When someone asks a question or drops some silly statistic I can reference the report and point to real data when answering. Much of the data that follows can be found in that report. I highly suggest downloading it before you start engaging in these conversations; it's hard to argue with the actual numbers.

"It's Not Addictive"

There is simply no arguing this fact: *marijuana is addictive*. Now, it is less addictive than plenty of other things, but establishing an addiction is not arbitrary. A person either meets the diagnostic criteria or does not. When diagnosing a substance use disorder (SUD) the following criteria is used:

1. Taking the substance in larger amounts or for longer than you meant to.
2. Wanting to cut down or stop using the substance but not managing to.
3. Spending a lot of time getting, using, or recovering from use of the substance.
4. Cravings and urges to use the substance.
5. Not managing to do what you should at work, home, or school because of substance use.
6. Continuing to use, even when it causes problems in relationships.
7. Giving up important social, occupational, or recreational activities because of substance use.
8. Using substances again and again, even when it puts you in danger.
9. Continuing to use, even when you know you have a physical or psychological problem that could have been caused or made worse by the substance.
10. Needing more of the substance to get the effect you want (tolerance).
11. Development of withdrawal symptoms, which can be relieved by taking more of the substance.

The *DSM-5* allows clinicians to specify the severity of the substance use disorder, depending on how many symptoms are identified. Two or three symptoms indicate a mild substance use disorder, four or five symptoms indicate a moderate substance use disorder, and six or more symptoms indicate a severe substance use disorder.

So there you have it, in the comfort of your own home you, too, can diagnose SUD! The criteria above hold true across the board for all substances; there is nothing special about weed.

The rates that we have for addiction associated with weed are over a decade old, therefore they are most likely on the low to very low side of things. With that said, about one out of every nine adults and one out of every six juveniles who use weed will, at some point, meet the diagnostic criteria for addiction to THC. We're not talking about opinion here, this is medicine.

"It's Just a Plant"

Well, we have a whole chapter about that, don't we! To summarize, it *was* just a plant but isn't today. This is a manufactured drug that is produced with the intent of getting people higher than is natural. They like to tell you how a body naturally has cannabinol receptors so God must have intended us to use it. The answer to that is that our bodies have receptors for all kinds of things that are naturally produced, but not at the same levels as a foreign substance put into our bodies like today's THC. Simply because we all have opioid receptors in our brains doesn't mean we need opiates to live a whole life.

"It's Safer than Alcohol"

This is one of the most nonsensical arguments imaginable but it gets traction. Is jumping out of a seven-story window safer than an eight-story window? Is getting hit by a truck worse than a car? They all have negative effects!

Alcohol is by far the most devastating substance in our country by almost every measurement imaginable; it is also far and away the most used. As use increases so does harm; it's a ratio not a percentage. Alcohol is also tightly regulated (with federal support) and legal. They are actually presenting a pretty solid argument for making alcohol illegal much of the time, not adding to the list of readily available intoxicating substances. Since nobody is going to make alcohol illegal again we have to deal with what we are going to do now. We are not required to deal with legalized weed/commercialized THC (unless you live in, so far, a select few states), like we are with alcohol. It is a bigger issue than whether to choose weed or alcohol. Alcohol harms some people and not others, same as weed, but this has little to do with the legal status and more to do with how many people are using the drug. Remember: increased access means increased abuse.

"Nobody Has Ever Died from Weed"

Another common mistruth. A more accurate statement is "nobody has ever *overdosed* and died from THC." Nobody has ever overdosed from cigarettes and died but would we say that tobacco has never killed anyone? Weed has killed plenty of people and, unfortunately, that list grows daily.

Richard Kirk's defense in the murder trial of his wife faults THC intoxication as the reason why he should get a lighter sentence. In essence, they said, "The weed made me do it." One hundred people died in Colorado in 2015 because someone high on THC hit them while driving. In addition to cumulative and driving deaths, there are fires, explosions, suicides (which hit an all-time high in 2015, incidentally), death of kids due to poor parenting or flawed product labeling decisions, homicides related to weed deals, etc.

Weed has never killed anyone in the same way that tobacco has never killed anybody and it's not the alcohol to blame when someone drives drunk and takes a life. In these ways, people die all of the time as a result of weed. Saying otherwise is playing a deadly game of semantics. It's short-sighted, and it mocks those who have died as a direct or indirect result of weed.

I just left an event at which a mother named Sally Schindel shared a gut-wrenching story about her veteran son Andy and the tragic loss of his life. Suicide is one of the hardest things to talk about and Mrs. Schindel did it with poise and compassion. I strongly encourage you to read her full story, it can be found many places online, Google: Sally Schindel, Andy's Story.

At the event I attended, she showed a picture of the actual note her son left before he took his life after a long battle with marijuana addiction. It read: "My soul is already dead. Marijuana killed my soul plus ruined my brain." She showed this note in his own handwriting that he penned before hanging himself. Read those words again and tell me that weed has never killed anyone. Better yet, drop Sally a note and tell her. She is easy to find, she spends her time fighting commercial marijuana in her home state of Arizona.

Now Google these names and show it to the kids and professors who tell you nobody has ever died from weed:

- ✓ Daniel Juarez
- ✓ Levy Thamba Pongi
- ✓ Kristine Kirk
- ✓ Luke Goodman
- ✓ Tom Dohse
- ✓ Gemma Moss
- ✓ John O'Brien
- ✓ Peyton Knowlton
- ✓ Andrew "Andy" Zorn (Sally's son)

"Traffic Fatalities in Colorado Are Down"

This is simplistic and inaccurate. They are down *overall* (thank you safer cars and less texting and driving) but *way up for stoned drivers*. Download that HIDTA report I mentioned because I can't include it all here and these numbers deserve to be understood (search "Rocky Mountain HIDTA Marijuana Report"). Not only do we test about less than half of all the drivers involved in a fatal accident, we don't always test them for THC. With that said the increase from 2012 to 2014 was 100 percent. Almost 100 people died on Colorado roads in 2014 because a driver was high on marijuana (MJ).

To give you an idea of how screwed up this stuff can get, here is an interesting story. Last year, I was invited to speak at the Vail Symposium; a super cool venue full of thoughtful people offering fascinating discussions on a wide range of topics. I was sharing the stage with Brian Vicente, one of the guys who wrote A64. Brian went first, and one of the focal points of his presentation was that traffic fatalities were down in the year since A64 passed. He made a big deal about this, saying fewer drunk drivers were on the road because they had all switched to weed; he pretty much touted weed as a traffic lifesaver. His perfect example of correlation and not causation was warmly received until I showed the slide below with the statistics from the HIDTA report. It reveals how ridiculous it is to say that weed makes for fewer traffic fatalities when, in fact, it had been cited as the factor in almost 100 traffic deaths the year prior.

While shocking, this data is only a small part of the real story when you keep in mind that only 47 percent of operators involved in traffic fatalities were tested at all for drug impairment. The sample showing the following was taken from less than half of drivers involved in fatal accidents!

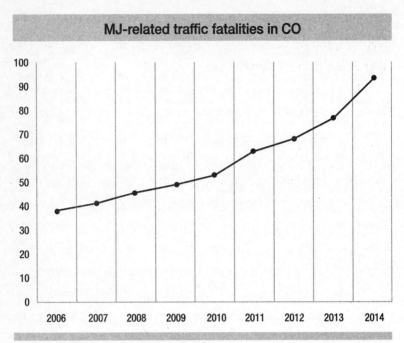

Source: Rocky Mountain High-Intensity Drug Trafficking Areas

✓ In 2014 (first year of retail), there was a 32 percent increase in marijuana-related traffic deaths.

✓ Marijuana-related traffic deaths increased 92 percent from 2010 to 2014, while all traffic fatalities in the same period rose only 8 percent.

✓ In 2009, marijuana-related traffic deaths, where the driver tested positive for THC, made up 10 percent of all traffic fatalities; by 2014, that had climbed to 19.26 percent.

Saying that our roads are safer today because we now have the highest past-month marijuana use between adults and youth in the country is just plain ignorant and an example of data manipulation that would get most "experts" laughed out of the room. For some reason, it seems to play in the narrative because there are so many well-paid people making the case. *Remember: their livelihood depends on passing off this fiction as truth.*

Since numbers often seem to do little to sway public opinion, let me give an example that will hopefully put a face on the data. In November 2014, Chad Britton, a local high school student, went out to his car at lunchtime to put a few things away. At just about the same time Brandon Cullip, another student from a different school, was in his car with friends getting high. Despite being warned by his friends that he was too high to drive, Brandon ignored them and slammed into Chad, killing him. Chad lost his life because Brandon got high and drove. This is another example of causation and not correlation.

Following the sentencing, Chad's father did an interview and said, "I think it was probably the worst thing that could happen to the state of Colorado, passing the marijuana law." The district attorney who prosecuted the case was quoted in the same article as saying, "The legalization of marijuana has supplied marijuana to kids and our youth and I don't think it's going to be the last time we have a tragedy like this because of marijuana."

I often hear driving while high made light of by the pro-THC side, saying how much better it is than driving drunk. They say that people are more cautious and therefore better drivers, a message that unfortunately many teens are hearing loud and clear. In reality, a 2015 study by the U.S. Department of Transportation found that marijuana users are twenty-five times more likely to be in accidents than those who did not use THC. And by way of comparison, drunk drivers are four times more likely to crash than sober drivers—there goes that theory!

There is one more important consideration to keep in mind when looking at this data: cops don't like to charge people with driving under the influence of weed. Since there is no breathalyzer or hard-line legal limit for THC, it can be very difficult to get a conviction for drivers who are high. Consequently, if there is anything else they can charge the driver with, they do.

You see, with alcohol it's simple: if a cop thinks you might be drunk they give you a breathalyzer. If you are over the legal limit of .08, you get arrested and charged with DUI. The case goes to trial, and with the blood alcohol level as evidence the driver is convicted and hopefully learns their lesson. The whole process is simple and straightforward.

With THC it's different. If a cop thinks a motorist is high they have to call in a drug recognition expert (DRE), a cop who is specifically trained in detecting drug impairment. That DRE arrives on the scene and puts the driver through a series of tests (taking up a good deal more of law enforcement's time than alcohol already at this point). If the DRE decides that the driver is under the influence of THC they try to get permission to draw blood. Since Colorado adopted a "limit" of 5ng/ml a blood test should be able to confirm if someone is "high" or not. And while Colorado does allow for the blood testing of any motorist thought to be intoxicated, it's a much bigger pain for the cops than having a person blow into a breathalyzer. The worst part is that having over the limit of 5ng/ml doesn't guarantee a conviction for DUID (driving under the influence of drugs) like testing over .08 does for DUI.

In March of 2016, a guy named Ralph Banks was arrested for DUID and tested at 7.9ng/ml, 2.9ng/ml higher than the "legal limit" in Colorado. The jury took less than thirty minutes to acquit him. Mr. Banks was able to retain Rob Corry, a big hired gun, to defend him. Rob played a pretty significant role in the passage of A64 and also likes to smoke weed. In September 2013, Rob was arrested at Coors Field for getting high in public as well as disobedience of a lawful order when he refused to give the officer, who he called a "stupid cop" the joint he was smoking. Rob knows THC law inside and out, in fact his website says "experience is key if you have been charged with a marijuana related crime." Rob clearly has experience!

Anyway, following the verdict Rob was quoted as saying, "Now with this case, it's perfectly legal to get behind the wheel after consuming marijuana as long as you're not impaired." Interestingly, multiple law enforcement officers, including a DRE, testified that Banks was impaired. The DA was then quoted as saying, "These are difficult cases to prosecute, but we continue to be concerned about the safety of the public. Our current law is not strong enough to effectively hold people accountable." Bad news, Mr. DA, because thanks to Rob and the defense he mounted for Banks, it just got a hell of a lot harder to get a conviction in spite of doing everything from an enforcement angle the right way. For more on this issue I strongly suggest looking into the work of the Foundation for Advancing Alcohol Responsibility and, specifically, the work of Erin Holmes, the Director of Public Safety.

"Crime Is Down in Colorado"

This little bit of data manipulation is one best left to the pros, the pro THC attorneys, and The Lobby. There are lots of ways to measure crime data, and if you pick them apart there is one possible way to argue that "crime is down" in Denver between 2013 and 2014. If you look only at "property crimes" you will see a 3 percent decrease. If you look at all crimes, including crimes against persons, crimes against society, and the catch-all "all other crimes," you will see an increase of 10 percent in one year. When you look specifically at marijuana-related crime in Denver, you will notice that there were 223 "crimes" in 2012, 239 in 2013, and 272 in 2014, another solid increase. My personal favorite is citations for public consumption of weed in Denver. Even with all of the alternative forms of consumption like edibles and vapes, we see that citations for using in public went from 8 in 2012 to 770 in 2014. Now, does that sound like freeing up police time to focus on more important things or does it look like handcuffing them to weed crimes so they can focus on little else?

"Look at All of the Tax Dollars!"

When we hear that weed tax collections amounted to $44 million in 2014 and about $135 million in 2015, our collective jaws drop; those appear to be big numbers! When you consider that our state operating budget for 2015 was $27,133,501,093 tax revenues of $135 million, less than half a percent of the budget, suddenly get a lot smaller. Think of Dr. Evil in the second Austin Powers movie saying they are going to extort "one million dollars" and everyone just looks at him—it's really not that much money. To you and me, $135 million is a *pile* of money; to a state government it's a rounding error.

The retort from The Industry is "It's money kept out of the black market." The retort to that retort is "No, it isn't." Since so many more people are using, thanks to the business marketing machines, that money would have likely been spent on other things that people needed more than weed, like diapers and what not. This point can be illustrated by the bill that was passed in Colorado in September 2014, called the "no welfare for weed" bill. This legislation restricted the use of government welfare cards being used at ATMs inside of weed shops. *The Industry is driving use, not the other way around.*

The real bottom line, and the reason why John Hickenlooper, our governor, is to this day telling other states not to legalize commercial THC for the money, is that you need that money to pay for the harms caused by the proliferation of the drug. Think of it like stepping out in front of a truck so that you can get the insurance money to pay for your injuries; doesn't make a ton of sense, does it? Because there are so many more harms being caused in our society because of the widespread use, we need more money to mitigate them. Law enforcement, treatment for substance use and related mental health issues, plus regulation are just a few of the costly hidden expenses. While some localities might actually net money from weed taxes, the state as a whole will lose big. It's a classic example of stepping over a dollar to pick up a dime, or more realistically, stepping over a ten-dollar bill to pick up a nickel.

"The Drug War Has Failed"

This one has to be the loudest argument in favor of legalization right now, and it seems like everyone is saying, "We all know that the war on drugs has failed." Lately, I'm hearing that almost daily and this argument makes me nuts! I'm going to stick to the spirit of this chapter and give you a simple retort for the seventeen-year-olds and professors with ponytails, but first I need to vent. It isn't even an argument; it's a statement given as fact that alienates differing viewpoints with the "everybody knows" bit. How dare we disagree with something so obviously true! One must be either stupid or just plain ignorant to not understand what "everybody knows." *Claiming this narrative as fact removes the opportunity for discussion, and that is ignorant.* In fact, everybody *doesn't* know that the war on drugs has failed and how, on God's green earth, could anyone ever substantiate such a statement *by relying solely on opinion and anecdotal examples.* It's like the woman who once started a question following a talk I gave by saying, "It's a given that drug abuse prevention has failed in this country." Says who? It's impossible to know what the world would look like without prevention (thank God). Likewise, we can't say the war on drugs has failed because there is no definition of winning that war short of a 100 percent substance-free society. Bad news there, that won't ever happen.

The phrase is wrong and even though I wasn't alive when it was coined, it's my understanding that President Nixon called the combination of enforcement, education, prevention, and education a "war." That was probably, in retrospect, pretty silly but that administration had its reasons: it was an all-out effort to eradicate drug use and abuse, and their resultant problems and cost to individuals and society. Nixon had declared drug abuse "public enemy number one." Maybe the administration was trying to convey the extreme importance of the issue to the public, using the strongest language they could in hopes of preventing more death and destruction; who knows. The problem with using that language, nearly fifty years later, is that it leaves us all wondering what the plan is to exit that war. My generation has spent lots of time thinking about those kinds of things politically in recent years. But if total victory in the drug war is not realistic how should we approach it? I guess we begin by settling for a less-than-perfect world, but I would rather live in a world that tries for the best possible outcome than one that throws in the towel because perfection eludes us. Some people I hang out with encourage us to pursue progress rather than perfection. That's good advice. Should we abandon the war on speeding because we don't have 100 percent compliance, or the war on car theft, robbery, terrorism, white-collar theft . . . you get the picture. Should we stop fighting those things or just say, "Screw it!" because we haven't gotten it perfect?

Let me pose a question: What would it look like if we abandoned the "enforcing drug laws" and called it that rather than a "war"?

I'm reminded of a line by one of my favorite poets, 2Pac, who essentially said we're waging the wrong war—one on drugs instead of on poverty. He was both right and wrong at the same time. *Poverty* is *the real issue* and we should stop treating the symptoms and do more to help those living in generational poverty to escape its cycle. He was misguided by proposing it as an either/or deal. Fighting drugs and fighting poverty could go hand-in-hand if anyone had the guts to take on something so complex. Earlier in that same song, he said that we weren't ready to have a black president. While the nation wasn't ready back in 1996 we are now, with Barack Obama who made it through two terms in the nation's highest office. It was about time we had a non-rich-white-guy president, and so much good has happened as a result, but he blew it on drug policy. While saying almost nothing, a new industry has sprung to life hell-bent on expanding use and taking money from our society's most vulnerable. I can't help but consider and mourn for the opportunity missed by a man so looked up to by youth and minority communities. With a few words, he could have changed the perception of hundreds of thousands of people for years to come and reduced the harms created by drugs in those communities. Instead of taking anything that resembled a leadership stance on drug use, he joked about getting high in school. Now I hear regularly that weed is a gateway drug to the White House. Considering an outlier as extreme as the president of the United States without considering the masses who have had their lives derailed, ruined or lost because of drugs is just nuts. Mr. Obama blew it on this front and his legacy will include what I believe will be seen as a mistake in years to come. He is the president who gave weed dealers a license to deal and traffic, mostly in the communities he says he cares most about. I wonder what he would do if he were raising his daughters alongside my kids in Colorado, would his stance have been the same?

Since I'm naming names I have to talk about Eric Holder for a second. That guy couldn't get out of office fast enough in my opinion. An attorney general does not get to pick and choose what laws they enforce based on how much they like the law. Their job is to uphold the laws of the land, not just the ones they dig. His actions and inactions on this issue have been devastating and the blame for many of the issues I've highlighted throughout this book lies at his feet. He should have to sit in a room with parents whose kids' lives were wrecked or lost in the last few years because of THC. That would get real pretty fast.

Now that I've gotten that off my chest we can go back to this talking point. Can you imagine what it would be like if we didn't try to stop drugs from coming into our country or to stop those dealing them from trafficking? Take a moment to consider life without enforcing these laws. Would the cartels be happy or sad if we stopped fighting them? How about the street dealers, who don't give a second thought to those who die using their products? Would they be depressed? I don't know about you, but I like that we fight back. I also don't believe that I know everything and choose to trust those we have appointed to protect and serve, to keep us safe. If law enforcement decides we should stop fighting drugs I'll reconsider, but for now I'm going to stand with our men and women in uniform and wish them safety and success fighting drugs and the devastation those drugs cause. I don't put my life on the line when I go to work every day but they do. We should not only listen a bit more to them, but we should tip our hats when they walk by rather than sneer. There are bad eggs in any field, law enforcement included, but for the most part these are some of the most honorable and upstanding men and women I know, who genuinely care about the communities they serve, and I'm going to stand behind them.

So how do we answer the question at hand? I would start with another question: "War is a bad term, are you proposing that we stop enforcing the laws?"

If that doesn't work ask them to define "war." I only do this to the ponytail types because it's kind of mean. Ask for some specifics about what the "war on drugs" is and watch the squirming. It's as hard to define and qualify as anything out there and individual talking points are easily countered. If all else fails ask a follow-up question: "How will we determine if any new approach has succeeded or failed; what would you measure?" Would you consider . . .

✓ **Locking people up?** We seldom do that with low-level offenders, so do you think we should stop punishing traffickers? Is it substance specific? How about somebody who gets caught a dozen times, do they need help? How can we get them that help without a legal stick? This country has a long history of locking too many people up, sometimes for very silly things, but we typically incarcerate people for doing bad things while being intoxicated and not for simply possessing a small amount of anything for personal use.

✓ **Locking up minorities?** Agreed, that sucks! Why do we do it for all crimes? Could it be we have more of an issue with poverty and racism than drugs? Is disproportionate incarceration confined to just drugs? The answer is that it is not, and I for one would like to see a much more substantive conversation taking place about root causes.

✓ **Spending money that could be spent elsewhere . . . where?** Would you use it for more treatment to counter the *huge* increase there would be in use, if it could be done with impunity? Would you use the dollars to pay for all of the tow trucks we would need to move the cars that people smash driving wasted because we stopped enforcement? Since intoxication often leads to poor decisions we would need that money to clean up the messes made by more intoxicated people making poor decisions. Maybe we could just give the money we weren't spending on enforcement directly to China. If our kids grow up higher on weed and their kids grow up studying harder who do we think will be the boss?

This argument makes no logical sense because we will never know what the world would look like today without the enforcement of the last several decades, and I think that's a good thing, with the exception of a mentality that seems to exist in some places that we should incarcerate everyone who makes a mistake as well as the examples out there of senseless enforcement and overzealous cops/prosecutors. Do you want to really take a bite out of the cartels? Let's start by getting less high in this country and reducing the demand that they will kill in a heartbeat to supply.

"It's Medicine"

For some people it might have medicinal benefits but that is a small group of very sick people. Medicines are double blind, placebo-control tested. If you want to say that it's medicine then treat it as such, with testing and regulations—*real* regulations. Medicines can be dangerous if you're not careful, and the side effects can be very real.

"Legalization Is Inevitable, We Might as Well Get in Line with It"

I was talking to a reporter recently about my opposition to any more weed shops in the city where I live. She told me that a city council member had just told her, "We already have two [shops] so what's the harm in adding more?" This makes about as much sense as, "Well, we have two inches of water in the house, what's the difference if we get another thirty?"

This guy, like so many others, has bought into the "inevitability" argument, which is an old political trick. Ever wonder why we always introduce candidates as, "The next mayor . . . the next senator . . . the next president . . . "? People want to back a winner and once a candidate is perceived as the winner it often becomes a self-fulfilling prophecy. It's kind of Sociology 101 stuff, we all want to be on the winning team. It's also a convenient, albeit irresponsible, way to avoid making thoughtful decisions and taking responsibility for what happens.

Using a very slick bit of strategy, The Lobby started talking about how inevitable commercialized THC was after Colorado and Washington passed it. The press *loved* that. They ran with that idea like it was their own and pretty soon the whole conversation pivoted. Two states had passed commercialized THC, by rather narrow margins, and all of the sudden, according to commentators and analysts in the media, as well as pop culture icons, it was a matter of a couple of years before the country followed suit and then most of the world!

This is political strategy not real prediction. Since 2012, here is what has actually happened:

- ✓ Oregon and Alaska passed recreational THC bills (paid for and built by the DPA). Both are in the process of implementing commercial sales.
- ✓ The District of Columbia passed true decriminalization without commercialization.
- ✓ Maine, Nevada, California, and Massachusetts just passed recreational laws and will be implementing them by 2018.

Recently much more has happened to contradict the inevitable narrative, but it just doesn't get the same press coverage nationally.

Ohio voted down commercialized THC as well as "medical" by a huge margin, by an almost two to one margin in 2016. In politics it is often said, "As goes Ohio so goes the nation." While this bill was pretty crazy from a commercial standpoint, it also included "medical" and it still went down in flames. This happened in spite of the millions spent by the "pro" side. Ohio failed; "As goes Ohio so goes the nation?"

Missouri turned down a loose "medical bill." Georgia, Utah, and Idaho all refused to allow for expanded CBD, passing only "medical" bills, despite tons of pressure.

Vermont didn't move forward and a lot of states are wisely sitting back and watching Colorado. If we are the canary in the coal mine, everybody had better give us more time to see if we turn up singing, coughing, or dead.

In 2015, Florida voters narrowly rejected a constitutional amendment legalizing the use of "medical" marijuana, the details of which were totally insane. Thankfully, enough people saw through that one because, had they passed it, it would have basically created a totally unregulated market overnight. Another piece of good news since that amendment provision died: the police continue to *not arrest* sick and dying people who smoke a bit of weed.

The reality is that the low hanging fruit has been plucked by the DPA and is being eaten by The Industry. We will continue to see more rejections than adoptions of THC commercialization moving forward as the data coming out of Colorado gets harder and harder to square up with and people in Wyoming (and other conservative states) consider these laws as opposed to people in Oregon (and other liberal and libertarian states). At some point the media will have to reflect the reality. Who knows, maybe Arianna Huffington will get a new board position, maybe with MADD or something.

If it is inevitable, why have so many more states rejected it than accepted in the last five years? It was inevitable that it happen somewhere given the money that was being spent, but people will wait to see the data coming out of these places over the next several years before any big changes take place across the nation. Given the early numbers we are seeing, it's pretty unlikely that many other states will follow suit. The low-hanging fruit has been plucked, passing recreational laws in Colorado will prove much easier than in Utah, in California than in Texas, and in Maine as opposed to Virginia.

Listed below are some organizations worth checking out:

✓ **Parents Opposed to Pot** (www.poppot.org)

A website that consists of (mostly parents) people who are opposed to the legalization and social acceptance of marijuana for the many reasons noted in this book. The website contains information and articles on the dangers of marijuana, including marijuana-related deaths among youths. Provided are testimonials from parents who have children addicted to marijuana.

✓ **Pueblo for Positive Impact** (Facebook page and www.propuebloco.com)

   An advocacy group in Pueblo County, Colorado (now recognized as the marijuana capital of Colorado) that opposes the legalization of marijuana and the dispensaries that have cropped up in their county. It provides statistics on the dangers of marijuana use, and also posts articles about marijuana and crime-related stories linked to pot in Pueblo County.

✓ **Smart Approaches to Marijuana (SAM)** (www.learnaboutsam.org)

   Professionals in mental and public health. This bipartisan group does not condone either the legalization *or* the demonization of marijuana, but seeks to educate citizens on the science of marijuana and to promote health-first, smart policies and attitudes that decrease marijuana use and its consequences.

✓ **The Marijuana Report** (www.themarijuanareport.org)

   This website is published by National Families in Action (NFIA). The report is a news aggregator website that links browsers to daily news coverage of the marijuana story across the nation. They put out a monthly e-newsletter and are partnered with SAM. Their mission is to help leaders make informed decisions about marijuana policy, including public, company, and family policy.

Consider what the Dalai Lama has had to say about craving, desire, and addiction:

"Most of our troubles are due to our passionate desire for and attachment to things that we misapprehend as enduring entities."

"Self-satisfaction alone cannot determine if a desire or action is positive or negative. The demarcation between a positive and a negative desire or action is not whether it gives you an immediate feeling of satisfaction, but whether it ultimately results in positive or negative consequences."

"When we think carefully, we see that the brief elation we experience when appeasing sensual impulses may not be very different from what the drug addict feels when indulging his or her habit. Temporary relief is soon followed by a craving for more. And in just the same way that taking drugs in the end only causes trouble, so, too, does much of what we undertake to fulfill our immediate sensory desires."

"When you are discontent, you always want more, more, more. Your desire can never be satisfied. But when you practice contentment, you can say to yourself, 'Oh yes—I already have everything that I really need.' "

CHAPTER 13

Addiction and Recovery

Yeah, They Are Real Things

If I had to take you down the road of substance abuse, from first use to addiction, it would be this in a nutshell: it starts off fun, gets less fun, then scary, then necessary. Necessary isn't really scary or fun, it's just . . . necessary. That's the progression I see in the lives of addicts I serve and that I recall myself. Remember the old commercial that said, "Nobody wants to grow up to be a junkie"? That's so true. We don't start getting high because it sucks; it's fun at first. We don't consider the long term. If we did we would stop in our tracks, considering what it's like to dream about getting to rehab if we're lucky, or die young if we're not.

We just want to have fun, kill the boredom, relax, laugh, stop feeling, be accepted, impress the girl, show them we're more than they think, get back at them, shut our brain off, escape the shame, stop the pain—those kinds of things.

Nobody takes their first hit giving thought to what their last hit will look or feel like. If we did I think we would all be done after one time. I wish I could play a few tapes of people calling into rehab at the end of addiction asking and begging for help; or parents who cry openly with a complete stranger while talking about their kids; or people telling us about their best friends who have become strangers; or those who tell us how the person they fell in love with and their greatest joy in life was now the source of their deepest pain; or kids desperately trying to help their parents. The heartbreaking stories of addiction I've heard talk about the destruction of lives and communities, sometimes for generations.

Addiction doesn't end well. Like ever. There isn't a single person I know who came out of their addiction because things were going awesome. That's not how it works. Losing a job, legal trouble, losing your family, seeing/doing/having awful things done to you; these are typically the kinds of things that make people think about addressing their addictions. It takes serious motivation and perseverance for people to go through what it takes to not only *get* sober but to *stay* sober those first couple of years. It takes guts to say you're willing to try to stop and something much bigger than guts to stay stopped.

Because we all have an idea in our mind of what an "addict" looks like and because this book is about weed, I want to describe what a THC addict can look like. Many people can recognize alcoholism if you're around someone who is an alcoholic long enough. Unfortunately, many of you can recognize other forms of addiction; gaining that knowledge is never fun. It's wild, however, that many people don't recognize what THC addiction looks like. Please keep in mind that the only way to say for certain if someone is an addict is to have a professional diagnose him or her with substance use disorder (SUD), but there are things to look for.

I'm typing this on a plane coming back from South Carolina. I gave a talk at a university and was asked by a student at the end of my presentation if you could tell someone was using drugs by their social tendencies. The question was well-intentioned but I chuckled a bit. If we could determine who was using based on what they liked to listen to, I believe anyone who drove around with me for a couple of days would probably think I got high! So be careful not to judge based on these things but instead use common sense. Parents, especially, should make it their job to ask lots of questions and know what to look for.

Cannabis use disorder is a real thing, and is included in the *Diagnostic and Statistical Manual of Mental Disorders (DSM-5)*, the American Psychiatric Association's universal authority for those in the mental health field. According to the federal agency that tracks this stuff, the Substance Abuse and Mental Health Services Administration (SAMHSA), 4.2 million Americans over the age of twelve met the criteria for cannabis use disorder in 2015. Symptoms include the following:

✓ Disruptions in functioning due to cannabis use
✓ The development of tolerance
✓ Cravings for cannabis
✓ The development of withdrawal symptoms, such as the inability to sleep, restlessness, nervousness, anger, or depression within a week of ceasing heavy use
✓ Etc.

That's some of what defines a technical addiction to cannabis. Defining addiction isn't subjective. Like diagnosing any other disease, one either meets the diagnostic criteria or one does not. I get asked all the time, "Is weed *actually* addictive, is that a real thing?" The fact is that the only debate about this is the one put forth by The Lobby/Industry. It would be like asking if Wyoming really borders Colorado to the north. I don't have to answer that question with an opinion, in the same way I don't have to answer the addiction question with an opinion; THC/marijuana is addictive, and if a person meets the criteria they are clinically diagnosable as addicted to the substance. Now, it is *less* addictive than some other substances *but that reality is changing as we study it more and as the potency increases. The bottom line is that addiction to THC is a very real thing.*

What Does THC Addiction Look Like?

So now that we have covered the technical stuff, let's get into practical application. Traditionally, weed addiction has been pretty subtle. The way it manifests doesn't happen overnight and isn't typically a huge explosion. There are exceptions, of course, but for the most part addiction to this substance takes more time to manifest and doesn't do so in a fiery mess.

Frequency of Use and Potency

If anyone is using more than a couple of times a month that's a warning sign. *The younger someone is, the more concerned I would be about the frequency of their use.* Think of it like alcohol. If an adult was getting drunk more than a few times a month you might be concerned. Since nobody is using THC for the flavor or for any reason other than to get intoxicated, frequent use is something to watch for because it equates to frequent intoxication. Now if the person getting drunk is a kid, then a couple of times a month is a different story, it's more pressing. The same things apply with weed use.

If someone is using THC multiple times a week, pay close attention and ask some questions. What would happen if you stopped for seven days, thirty, sixty? If the answer is "No big deal, I do it all the time" then I would worry less. If the thought of stopping for a few days freaks somebody out and they push back hard or get angry, that would concern me.

In addition to frequent consumption, the potency of what people are consuming is worth considering in today's day and age. Someone using concentrates once a day is a pretty big deal; it might be equivalent to a person smoking regular 25 percent THC weed multiple times a day. Just think of it simply: too often/too strong should give us pause.

Reasons for Use

People will often talk about benefits of use when in reality many are telling us about symptoms of withdrawal rather than benefits of using. *The benefit is that consumption keeps the withdrawal symptoms at rest.* We're going to talk about withdrawal in a second, don't freak out yet! Being anxious and nervous when you stop consuming are withdrawal symptoms as well as trouble sleeping and feeling nauseated.

When someone tells me that they need THC to sleep, I know that's real; they may very well be experiencing subtle symptoms of withdrawal. It sounds kind of backwards, right? Lots of stuff that isn't good for your body will make you go to sleep.

The Challenges of Confronting a THC Addict

One of the most challenging things recently has been people who clearly meet the diagnostic criteria of cannabis use disorder telling us that they aren't addicted because one can't be addicted to weed. I actually saw a nineteen-year-old patient arguing with an addiction-specific physician whose career is working with substance use disorder. The patient was telling the doctor that she had it all wrong, weed wasn't an issue because it isn't addictive—and he was in rehab.

People seem to recognize that if they can't stop using other substances, and if those other substances are having very negative effects on their lives, they might have an issue. It seems harder to have that talk with people today about weed, especially younger people who are so much more vulnerable, identity conscious, and easily manipulated. With that in mind, realize that talking to people who might be addicted to THC can be pretty challenging.

Keep in mind that if someone really is addicted to something, they aren't excited about it. They might be resolute on the outside about it being no big deal, or a choice, or a necessary medicine, or a way to find their identity, but if my experience is any indication, that person wants out even if he or she can't say it or imagine being out. My friend Keith, the interventionist I mentioned earlier, sums it up best. People are always telling him how tough their loved one is going to be and that they will never agree to treatment. Keith says this, "I know a secret, because I've been there. I know that deep down inside they don't want to live like this. They just can't imagine anything else but they hope for it even if they don't know what it (sobriety) looks like."

THC Withdrawal

A full discussion of withdrawal is so crucial and important when considering the direction we are heading that I almost gave it a chapter of its own. It is such a big deal that I talk about this in the first few minutes of almost every talk I give.

For the first time ever, cannabis withdrawal was included in the latest edition of the *Diagnostic and Statistical Manual of Mental Disorders (DSM-5)*, the American Psychiatric Association's universal authority for those in the mental health field. The fifth revised version of this manual came out in 2013 and includes signs and symptoms, as well as diagnosing criteria for cannabis withdraw. This is *the* manual for this stuff. It's not a political document or opinion, it's a medical diagnostic criteria developed by experts in the field.

Withdrawal from weed wasn't included in the previous four versions because it was so rare, if it existed at all. This is such a key part to understanding THC today compared to the weed of years gone by. At 4 percent THC, people weren't detoxing from weed, they just stopped. When Willie Nelson started smoking weed he could have put it down without much consequence. In all likelihood, it would be very different for him to stop today. *Because it's so much stronger today, it affects the human body much more than before.* Coming down off of weed isn't going to kill you like alcohol or benzos can, and isn't going to have you on the floor in the same way that opiates do, but it can really be miserable. It is also very unpredictable. Because of the way THC metabolizes in our bodies it tends to hang around much longer and sometimes come back around when someone thought they were all detoxed and clean. We can do a pretty good job predicting how a person will detox from almost all substances, but THC is an exception. We are getting better at it but THC is really unpredictable and there are no medications to aid in the detox process from weed.

Indiana Jones is lame now. *Star Wars* sucked then got cool again. The Cubs finally won the World Series. Johnny Cash is gone. Cars are starting to drive themselves. People are having to detox from weed. What's the world coming to?

Addiction can look very different on different people so consider the things above and ask a professional if you have questions. If you go to a doctor, you should probably look for one who is certified by the American Society of Addiction Medicine (ASAM) or American Board of Addiction Medicine (ABAM). If a therapist, find someone who works regularly with addiction. There are plenty of people who can help.

Why We Get High— Continued

I gave a partial list earlier of why people feel the need to get stoned, or at least a partial list of things that influenced my use. However, this is such a big question that people have dedicated their lives to researching it, and we could fill several books with what we know and still not get it all down. The reasons are as diverse as the individuals who use and many of them apply to a variety of substances. It's more about the person than the substance. I know guys who use porn for many of the same reasons I used drugs and drank. Some people use food or exercise the same way. It's about the person not the substance. The unhealthy and often dangerous behaviors sometimes make sense when you understand a person's history.

Since this is a book about weed, I'm going to stick to that when answering the *why we use* question. Given all of the reasons mentioned earlier there are some things specific to weed and specific to weed in Colorado that deserve special mention.

People use because they are told and believe that weed/THC is harmless. There is such an effort to convince us that it's a lesser evil or not an evil at all that people are starting to believe it. We are told that it's safer than alcohol and, unlike other drugs, that it has never killed anyone (see Chapter 7). It's interesting to consider who is giving us that message. It's not the American Medical Association (AMA), not the American Society of Addiction Medicine (ASAM) or the American Psychiatric Association (APA). *It's a message brought to us by the guys lobbying for the sale of the drug. Economics, not science, has driven this message.*

People use because it's easy to get. We know that the easier the access, the more people will access it. Weed is easier to get than meth, so more people use weed. Alcohol is easier to get than weed, so more people use alcohol than weed. This is a simple observation that holds true across any example. If there are eighty-plus more dispensaries in Denver than there are McDonald's and Starbucks combined, then does that mean it's easier to get a joint and a THC cookie than a latte and a burger?

People use because they are told to and are pressured to. The less people are exposed to a thing and the less they are encouraged to use that thing the less they will use it. It's that simple. Ask yourself if the advertisements below are "exposing and encouraging"?

SWEET LEAF
marijuana centers
Smoke
WEED
Everyday
WITH THE SWEETEST DAILY DEALS IN TOWN

The Culture

One of the smartest and most compassionate people I know in the treatment field is Dr. LaTisha Bader. Dr. Bader and I did a talk together a year ago for a bunch of sports psychologists in Big Sky, Montana, about THC. As Dr. Bader and I were preparing the presentation, she shared a chart with me highlighting several areas of culture that are influenced by addiction as well as recovery. We used it in our talk to show how recovery and addiction can look in regard to THC use. Those areas are highlighted in the list below:

- ✓ Language
- ✓ Food
- ✓ Music
- ✓ Religion
- ✓ Sex
- ✓ Family
- ✓ Literature
- ✓ Values

✓ Symbols   ✓ Leisure
✓ Rituals   ✓ Time
✓ Dress   ✓ Violence

All of these areas can be dramatically influenced by a person's drug use. What I'm increasingly seeing more of is the huge subculture around marijuana use. When you have pop-up ads for weed shops on the Internet every time you read a story about weed it should tell you something about the proliferation and normalization of a culture integrated around marijuana use. *What was once a countercul-ture is now a subculture, and if left unchecked will just be our culture.* Weed has its own magazines (way more than just *High Times*), radio shows, more websites than I could count, and now associations and trade unions. *The Denver Post,* Denver's major daily newspaper, has a specialty publication called *The Cannabist,* which it says addresses, "cannabis' ever-expanding role in our weekly lives via news cover-age, pot-rooted recipes, arts features, strain and gear reviews, lifestyle profiles, business articles and more, more, more." *The Post,* which had been struggling as were most daily newspapers, now gets big ad revenue from the numerous *Cannabist* advertisers. With the huge THC-based industry now driving its own culture, it is getting easier to become immersed in the overall drug culture. For many users it's become a second family, a group of people who not only accepts them but encourages them to go forward in their use and often discourages them from getting help. Even if their peers were to encourage them to stop using, the reality is that in addition to losing the substance they have come to rely on, people who quit getting high also stand to lose identity and community. While this exists with alcohol, marijuana is unique in that it has become so widely accepted, and many people are using it to establish their personal and social worlds and worldview. I've never seen a person wearing a hat about meth or heroin socks but see both featuring weed daily.

How to Help

Nearly every day, I'm asked what someone can do to help a loved one who is addicted to THC. The answers are as diverse as the people who ask. While every situation is different, one thing that can be said for everyone wishing to help is to lead with love and compassion. It isn't about shaming someone into wanting to stop or scaring them into it. Help must come from a place of love. When it comes from the heart, your caring will be evident and, as a result, it will be much easier for the person to hear. There are also times when one has to say "Enough is enough," then set boundaries and stick to them, no matter how hard that is.

A crisis can help a person be more willing to get help but avoid talking to a loved one in crisis, if it can be avoided. For example, if your loved one comes home high and you have already been talking about his or her substance abuse, you will likely be pretty angry. If you're not careful, trying to help when you're upset stands to be more about you than them. We tend to react when we're upset and those emotions can make the conversation that needs to happen much harder. As opposed to getting into it when you're fired up, consider giving it a day and having that talk when things are going well. Sitting down to a meal together the next day might help your message be heard and help you come into the conversation with a level head, more capable of delivering that message out of love and compassion than anger. This isn't to say that emotion is a bad thing when talking to someone about their use. It wouldn't be real to try to do it free of emotion. Just consider how you can best do it out of a place of love over anger, those messages are often heard better by the addict.

The most effective thing you can do is to enlist the help of a professional. There are some amazing people out there. The right interventionist and treatment center can be a true lifesaver. There are lots of people out there so choose carefully. Don't be fooled by slick sales pitches and flashy websites, ask some hard questions. You can also talk to your doctor and ask for referrals to physicians who specialize in addiction.

This can be a really tough thing to do so don't do it alone. Get other people who know what they're doing and enlist their help. You can also ask someone you know who has been sober for a while for help, we love the opportunity to help out in times like these.

Of course, if there are any circumstances that make you think a person's use is immediately life threatening, that whole waiting for the right moment thing goes out the window. Get help right away and do whatever it takes to help.

The hardest news very well may be that even if you do everything perfectly there are no guarantees you will be heard or that treatment will be "successful." I'm asked all the time what will do it, what will "fix" a loved one from their addiction. The reality is that there isn't a formula that works every time. There are so many factors and ways to help that it might be beneficial to look at it like stacking the right blankets on somebody who is freezing. If you stack enough and if they are the right kind, the odds improve with every blanket. We want to give the addict every opportunity to "warm up" that we can. The thing that is so hard to communicate and to hear is that there are no guarantees, and anyone who is telling you otherwise is just giving you a sales pitch—there is no silver bullet. So many things can help, and the right combination of those things (meds, support groups, therapy, treatment, behavioral interventions, monitoring, exercise, etc.) can give the addict a very good chance; but not a guarantee.

I spoke to a friend this week whose story helps to make this point. She has been through the ringer with THC addiction in her family. She has a perspective that I don't often see; she has set boundaries to protect her family, loves her son very much, and continues to show that love and offers help to him. She speaks openly about her experiences and offers help to others in similar situations. She is an inspiration and a great example of how doing all we can sometimes doesn't produce the results we are hoping and praying for. I'm going to share a bit of their story, beginning with how her son was first exposed and how things progressed. But this is mostly a story about how to help. The names have, of course, been changed, and changed awesomely might I add. I've had my name changed in a few books and they always come up with something *way* lame, not this time!

Shera has two sons and was career military. She went on to work for a charity helping veterans when they left the service when she retired. She is charming, well spoken, smart, and the kind of person people just like being around. She is also someone who knows what it's like to be sick. In fact, she was diagnosed with two of the chronic and life-threatening conditions that many claim can be cured by weed. Being someone who relies on doctors rather than budtenders, she is treating these illnesses traditionally and not getting high.

Shera speaks often of her son, Bosco, both publicly and privately. I have never seen her do so without class and respect for him as a person, which is refreshing in this conversation. Bosco has been in and out of recovery and is also very open about his struggle.

He started getting high in junior high school and hit it pretty hard. The weed was easy to get, mostly from the parents of friends or people who had med cards. Early on in high school, Bosco discovered "dabbing" and things got pretty bad for him pretty quickly. As we discussed in the chapter on concentrates, this stuff is nasty and we don't know what it's doing to people's brains, and especially in the brains of teens. It is bad news and this form of marijuana doesn't have a place in the world.

Because of a variety of factors, including tolerance to THC, cultural acceptance, and availability, Bosco was using concentrated THC regularly, sometimes even more than twelve times a day. His parents sought help through the military healthcare system. After a few visits with a doctor doing talk therapy at the VA, Bosco was told that he needed inpatient rehab to address his addiction to THC. He responded like most young people do, telling the mental health professional that a person can't get addicted to weed. But he capitulated and went to rehab anyway.

When Bosco left rehab he was fired up and did well for a bit. He even talked publicly about how the culture made it so easy for him to get high. He spoke about getting his med card after telling a doctor he had a knee injury from football (he never played), and how the doc bent his leg a few times and gave him the approval. He described how afterward, as a card-carrying "patient," he was in high demand. Being signed up with a "caregiver" would allow that person to grow lots of additional plants to supposedly support his "treatment."

According to Colorado law, a patient can only change caregivers once a month, but Bosco did it all the time. He was a patient at most of the medical dispensaries in his town. This is illegal, of course, but the letters the state sends telling you to knock it off aren't worth the

How many doctors that you know hold "patient drives"
to drum up business?

Since demand is so high for "patients" the perks one gets with a red card
go way past not having to pay taxes. Readily available is free weed, free
pipes, free weed, clothing, free weed, buy one get one deals, free weed,
contests, free weed, food, and barbecues—and did I mention free weed?

paper they are written on. He was very frank about how the culture aided his addiction, but The Industry was what allowed him, an eighteen-year-old kid, to get high all day, every day, at almost no cost. He became an expert at how to work the system and to clip coupons—literally clip coupons.

When Bosco came back from treatment he was ready to stay sober. He got a job delivering pizzas and was working to get his life back on track. As someone with a few years of sobriety, I can tell you that living in this kind of environment can be intense. For Bosco, the pressure was way intense. He would often be offered weed as a tip for dropping off a pizza; it's practically a currency here! And he was surrounded by stores, advertisements, the culture of gratification and abuse, and the sheer smell of it. The challenges proved too much to resist in his early recovery. Bosco ended up relapsing and is currently living in a "gray market" grow house. It basically functions as a co-op where a group of people are growing their legally allowed six plants each, but in the same place. There are many more people on the books than are actually growing weed. This kind of arrangement makes large-scale growing kind of legal-ish should they get raided.

Bosco has had a rough go of it, and it's one that I intimately understand myself. Shera also has had, and continues to have challenges along the way, too. Since my experience is only that of the addict, I asked Shera what she thought other parents might benefit from hearing.

Everything she said came back to her love for Bosco, as well as for her husband and other son. She is clearly motivated by family. She shared some of the family traditions they kept, what it was like in their home, and how much she cared for her boys.

Shera told me that if she could do it again, she would have paid closer attention to the families of Bosco's friends. There were instances when those parents were disconnected from their children and times when some of them actually shared weed with the kids. She wishes she had known those families better at the beginning before allowing Bosco to spend time there. As a parent of three young children, I know how awkward it can be when you tell a parent that your child can't go over until we all get some time together. It's hard for them to think they're not trusted, but we don't automatically assume all parents are trustworthy. Until we know somebody, we don't know them. In addition to asking about guns in the house and allergens (we have a few severe ones), we now ask about THC, especially edibles. Talking to Shera reinforced the importance of having these conversations.

She also said that she wished she had encouraged more extracurricular activities. Bosco was in ROTC for a time but other than that wasn't involved in anything else. She now thinks that sports, clubs, or other healthy endeavors could have been a big help. But her bottom line was the importance of knowing friends and their families.

Shera and her husband had to ask Bosco to leave the house a while back. It was totally appropriate, agreed upon in advance, and even spelled out in a contract, but that didn't make it easy. She continues to encourage Bosco and try to help him but they have also set up boundaries to make sure that their lives stay as manageable as possible in the midst of his unmanageable addiction. In a world that could use more love and more loving families Shera and her family are examples to me of how to do it well. I am optimistic about Bosco's chances for recovery because he doesn't want to get stoned. Although he can't stop right now, it is his desire to quit using that gives me hope. His family isn't giving up hope either, and they also aren't accepting the nonsense going on out there in the free marketplace. Shera is vocal about how The Industry influenced Bosco and his life, and she is making her voice heard in the hope that other families can avoid the same things. Keep yelling, my friend, people will listen eventually. I hope it's sooner than later.

Recovery

Getting sober is kind of the opposite of addiction; it starts out tough, gets really intense and then is one of the most rewarding things in life. It's not easy to get sober. As anything that is worthwhile, it takes effort, grit, and determination. They say that the only thing you need to change in recovery is everything. Changing everything is rough! It's also totally necessary. We all know plenty of people who don't use anymore and aren't anyone we want to be around; it has to be more than not using. Getting sober is much more than just *quitting* something, it's about *starting* something. Sobriety involves starting to deal honestly with the world, starting to look hard at what our motivations are, starting to ask hard questions, considering the answers, and developing a willingness to start changing everything.

While the early days of sobriety are difficult, being sober is amazing. We gain clarity that would have been impossible and unimaginable when we were high. Connection with others and with a higher power has been one of the most rewarding parts for me. Not only is it easier to be present and live in the moment, I've found an acceptance of circumstances that I just didn't have before. We are told that to stay sober we need to learn to accept life on life's terms. While that doesn't mean taking things lying down, it does mean that we come to realize that it's not all about us, and that we need to allow others into our lives.

At the risk of sounding a bit cheesy, recovery isn't a destination, it really is a journey. For those who love us and want to see us sober, what they are usually hoping for is that we stop getting high, not so much that we start doing all of those other things, it's hard for them to see past the immediate. Getting sober isn't really about not getting high but it starts there. If we were to stop at just not getting high anymore we would be a pretty rough crowd. So much has to be removed from our lives and changed, it needs to be replaced with something. Hopefully, that's something healthier.

What It Looks Like

My first two years of recovery were really tough. I was only seventeen but had dug myself a pretty deep hole. I had all kinds of identity issues once I stopped using and, basically, I was a hot mess. I didn't know how to act around people or how to go to sleep. When I did sleep, I dreamed about getting high and drunk just about every night, some of them so realistic that I woke up thinking I had relapsed. Having to feel for the first time in several years was probably the biggest shock. Being intoxicated mutes emotions in the same way it amplifies Yanni's new age music (he is pretty hard to dig sober isn't he?). I had grown accustomed to not feeling that which wasn't physical, so when I started feeling my emotions again, it seriously freaked me out and I stuffed them deep down inside. The intensity of feeling again can be overwhelming. Keep that in mind if you are just getting sober or someone you love is new in recovery.

There were a few things that saved my tail in those first two years when things felt so rough. The first was fear. I was terrified of going back once I stopped. I lost three very close friends to addiction/intoxication in that time and another was sent to prison for a term of twenty-five years to life. The stakes were high and I was reminded of them often. Before I got sober, I can honestly say that I had no real interest in being alive other than the basic biology of it. I didn't want to die but I didn't really care to be alive. When I got sober there were days—which increased in frequency the longer I stayed sober—where I *really did* want to be alive. A buddy describes getting sober as walking out of a really crappy matinee movie into a bright sunny afternoon, you feel so hollow when you walk outside, into reality. Until I was able to stop squinting and actually see the sun, lots of fear kept me from going back out. Thankfully, I will never know if this is true or not, but at the pace I was going and seeing what happened to most of my peer group, I doubt I would have made it another year; two would have been a very outside chance. For the first time in years, I knew that I not only didn't want to die, I was getting interested in living again.

Another saving grace was the twelve-step program that I attended. I had something to put my energy into: I went to a ton of meetings! After doing court-ordered meetings—lots of them—and attending a bunch as a kid with a family member, I knew my way into "the rooms" but hadn't ever gone there to work. My first two years I probably averaged eight meetings a week. Being around those people gave me the accountability that I needed, and it even gave me a little hope from time to time. I also had a few buddies who helped: Mike, Jay, Heath, and Doug saved my life more than once, and I'm forever grateful to them.

I also set a couple of goals early on that were a big help. I decided that I was going to finish high school and I made plans with three sober guys my age to travel the country as soon as I finished. Only two of us had our diplomas, and at age nineteen I was the last. Having the trip to look forward to and planning it with other guys in recovery was motivation in itself. When I finished school, we took off and spent the next three months driving. I got to see much of the country while living out of a car/tent and fell in love with Canada and Alaska. I actually celebrated my two years sober on that trip.

After that milestone it got much better, and I started to find some identity and peace again. I won't go into all of it—this isn't the place for that—but just like there were a few things that kept me sober at the very beginning, there were a few things that helped me make it those next crucial few years. I reconnected spiritually and went to work trying to understand what that looked like in my life. I had some dear friends who didn't use and who played a big role in helping me create that new identity. If not for late nights playing basketball and building fires I don't think I would have enjoyed those years nearly as much. Ben, Sammy, and Jon showed me what it was all about; I learned how to laugh again with them.

I also got super lucky and fell in love with the most amazing person I've met to this day. Christy gave me the final push I needed to want to live more than to be afraid of dying. With her, my life started to take on color. After gritting my teeth through the beginning, sober years two to five were actually beautiful. I felt like a kid (albeit one with a rough past who knew how to steal cars) learning about the world for the first time. It was a time of self-discovery and then of emotional awareness that I hadn't experienced since childhood. All of this was topped off by falling in love and marrying someone who I can't even imagine not having as my partner. My wife is the most inspiring person I have ever met and she motivated me to keep on working and growing.

The literature calls over five years "late-stage recovery." It's when we're supposed to have it all together—ha! While you do have the tools to stay sober and keep growing as much as you're willing to work for, life doesn't stop happening and that means things can get really hard at points. I had a couple of those points in 2006, 2009, and 2012. These events were notably painful. Fortunately, I had the tools I needed to stay sober, and I had enough people who understood what I was going through in my life so I could process those things and try to integrate them into my life over time. Life won't stop dealing us pain when we get sober; that is just part of the tradeoff we have to make for being alive. But the pain can be dealt with and processed so that we don't destroy our lives or those of the people around us. Heck, if you can manage it like a few guys I know, that kind of stuff can actually make you a better person.

There is no certificate of graduation from addiction. There won't come a day when I finally say, "Well, beat that one good, what's next?" I will always have to work on stuff to stay sober, but the big difference today is that it isn't something that I dread. I like living this way, and I want to continue learning and growing as long as I'm able. I'm glad that I will have the recovery community around me for whatever life hands me next.

With that said, my addiction and my recovery are less of my identity than they were in the beginning, and for me that feels right. I will always be an addict/alcoholic, but I am much more than that today. After twenty years of sobriety, those parts of my identity make up more of me than does the addiction. Before the identity of "addict," I see myself as a husband, father, community member, productive member of society, climber, fisherman—that kind of stuff. It's not that the addiction stops being there, it's just under layers of other things today. So for me, that's what it looks like. Seeing the change that takes place at the beginning is a big part of why I do what I do professionally. People walk in the doors hopeless and lost. We can help them find what they need to get sober and restore hope. Watching that transformation is unparalleled.

How to Start

Earlier I spoke to the person who has a loved one they are concerned about. This part is for those of you who think or know that you personally might have a problem.

First things first, you have to ask yourself how bad is it? If your life is in danger, hit the panic button. Go to the ER, go to a physician, get into the care of medical professionals right away. Treating long-term addiction is a specialty, so this will likely be just a first step. But you can't get to step two if you're not alive. If it's life threatening don't screw around, get somebody who knows what they are doing to help you.

If it's not life threatening, let me encourage you to start out by hitting a meeting. There are so many meetings today that you're sure to find something that works. Try a couple until you connect with someone. The advantage to this is that it's free. You can go and start to look into all of this and it won't cost you the price of treatment. This isn't to say that treatment won't be necessary but let's cover that next.

Everyone is different and every meeting is different. Just like there is Alcoholics Anonymous and Narcotics Anonymous there is now Marijuana Anonymous. Check out a few meetings before you make your mind up. I hear people all the time say that they can't do twelve-step because of all of that God stuff. It's not like that, seriously, and if you go to a group where it is not what you want then just go to another! There are actually a few twelve-step groups that totally omit a higher power component.

While it might scare you to think about walking into a meeting, consider some of the crap you have done to get high or while high. Compared to all of that, this is nothing! If you still feel too self-conscious, sit in the back and just listen. While some people will likely introduce themselves to you at some point, nobody will make you talk to the group if you don't want to do it.

Treatment is a very necessary and lifesaving thing for many people. Let's say you've abused your body or you have some mental health concerns that need professional help and maybe even medication. Treatment is a good thing, but make sure to pick a facility that is reputable; we can cover that later. Addressing those issues separately from the addiction can delay recovery on many fronts. *Addiction is another chronic disease and it needs to be treated as such. It needs to be dealt with alongside other illness, be they mental or physical.* The lack of respect for mental health disorders that people sometimes encounter is just a combination of ignorance and prejudice. My friend Patrick Kennedy, the former U.S. Congressman, is involved in the THC conversation because of his advocacy for mental health. He likes to say, "The brain is a part of the body," and it's about time this country starts to recognize that. It will make a big difference in our collective quality of life when we give as much attention to mental health as we do to physical well-being.

For some, getting medications right at the beginning is crucial if we're going to maintain sobriety and mental health. Doing that during inpatient care gives the medical professionals the ability to see you around the clock and to make adjustments to things in real time rather than once a month when you have an appointment. It also allows them to monitor just what is going on physically with you in order to help in more than just one way at a time. Sometimes, what helps in detox might not help later on and vice versa, so being in a place where you can be treated around the clock can take months or years off of the time it takes to get your body (brain included) back on track in early recovery.

Treatment is also good because it's a bit of a reprieve from the world. When your immediate needs are cared for (food, shelter, physical, etc.) it's much easier to focus on doing that critical work that should be performed early on. I can only assume that my first two years of "tough" might have been reduced to a month or two if I had been under professional inpatient care and was just working on the issues at hand and not all of the other distractions that can throw you off track.

The stakes are high when it comes to dealing with addiction so don't treat it lightly. While I always encourage the meetings first (they're free!) most people with substance use disorder do need some form of treatment, and everybody could benefit from working with a team of dedicated professionals for a time.

If the idea is still scary but you think it might be right, make a few calls and ask tons of questions. A good program will be willing to answer anything you throw at them and help determine what you need. You can also ask to tour a facility, and seeing a place firsthand is a great idea.

Getting care from other professionals not in an inpatient setting is also a strongly advisable option. If the idea of treatment still freaks you out, that's cool, just go see someone in their office. Be honest (you're paying them so you might as well get your money's worth) and see what they think the appropriate level of care is for you. If they ultimately recommend treatment you will have an ally to work with in finding the appropriate program. Make sure to find people who understand addiction and seriously, be honest with them. Nothing you're going to say will freak them out and they aren't there to judge you at all, just to help. Give it to them straight so they can help. Relationships with therapists/docs are professional relationships, this is what they do. It's not a friendship so use their knowledge to get well, don't worry about putting the best foot forward because that will probably slow it down in the end.

The "Other" Culture

I had to ask a couple of buddies about this one, "What is the culture of recovery?" It's a big question and I don't want to pretend to have the market cornered on this, even a little bit. I think it means lots of different things to people. There are, however, some common experiences and pieces of "culture" that lots of people seem to identify with being in recovery.

First of all, we're the best designated drivers ever! If you're lucky enough to have a friend in recovery you're probably loving life when they agree to go out on the weekend. I'm a bit older now and so are my buddies but for a couple of years I got those calls pretty regularly. They went something like this:

> Friend: Hey man, how's stuff?
> Me: You know, great.
> Friend: Small talk (typically Broncos, climbing or fishing related depending on the time of year).
> Me: Small talk right back (typically really witty and funny).
> Friend: *Sooooo,* what are you up to on Friday night? Wanna hang out?
> Me: Probably not but go ahead and ask.

Friend: Well, a bunch of us are going to go out to dinner and check out this show then maybe hang out downtown for a bit.
Me: Fine, I'll go but I eat for free and I'm not doing karaoke again with you losers.

In addition to being on-call designated drivers there are a few more things about the culture of recovery worth noting. We can be painfully self-aware at times, and some of us never grow out of it. Imagine being in a room where everyone says exactly what they are feeling in real time and it typically revolves around themselves. That can be a lot like being in a room with folks in recovery. It's not just about wearing our hearts on our sleeves; sometimes we straight up lob them around like grenades. The good news is that if we keep doing the work, this does ease up.

I also like to think that we are a little more willing to consider our own part in things and try not to blame people. We get so amazing at blaming others in addiction and especially early recovery. When we're living in addiction our own contributions to a problem elude us and we tend to see everyone else's shortcomings very well. For example, if you want to see the most entitled group of people on earth, let an addict be sober for like eight minutes and watch that show! Before they get "sober" they want all of the patience and understanding on earth, asking for one more chance, just one! Nothing was our fault and we can't believe that you can't believe us when we tell you:

✓ It wasn't mine.
✓ I was holding it for a friend.

- ✓ Someone must have put it into my drink.
- ✓ I told them to either put it out or crack a window, it must be secondhand.
- ✓ I swear to you, I didn't.
- ✓ I swear to you, I never will again.
- ✓ *They* are lying.
- ✓ I love you and would never do that.
- ✓ Don't you trust me?

Now flip the script to the addict who just got sober; we tend to demand absolute perfection from everyone around us:

- ✓ You're twenty-three seconds late! Clearly, you don't respect my time.
- ✓ Oh, you don't know where the meeting is! Well I wonder what they're paying you for "preacher"?
- ✓ What do you mean you don't believe me? You have no idea what I'm going through and what it took to get here.

But then something starts to happen. It's hard to say when because it can be way different for everyone; for me it was about two years into things but I've seen guys get it after a week or two. I think they were able to be more honest and transparent than I was back then.

We start to realize: maybe the world doesn't spin around us, that we might not be the center of everything. With that realization comes a freedom that is the beginning of the journey. If we stay on the path we start to get honest where we used to be less than honest, especially about who we are. If we are willing to be honest about what hurts we can start to heal and when we get to healing, the world hurts less and it becomes less about not getting high and more about living again.

The second chance at life makes it tough not to do much of what we do out of gratitude and maybe even grace for others. We realize that everybody is hurting and dealing with it in their own ways. My buddy Bobby likes to say that, "We're playing on house money," because we have no business being here after what we have done but we are. Playing on house money is pretty liberating.

Like I said, recovery looks very different to different people. For me, the greatest gift has been my ability to go through life with some measure of compassion, grace, and honesty. Doesn't mean I don't hurt, or fear or doubt, or screw up, I do. I just spend more time today on the former than the latter.

Afterword

It's Time We Started Really Paying Attention to This Weed "Experiment" in Colorado

As I come to the end of this book, I am left scratching my head and asking, "How are so many smart people missing this?"

When I was in the heavy research and writing phase of this project, I sequestered myself from just about all media. I cut out reading for enjoyment and watching much of anything that wasn't related to weed. To celebrate the finished manuscript, my wife and I rented a movie and planned a date night to watch *The Big Short*, the film about the credit and housing bubble collapse of the mid-2000s, fueled by greed and corruption. At the end of the film we were both sitting there thinking the same thing, she said it first: "It's the same thing as weed right now." My wife was referring to the housing market bust and how the entire world, with a few exceptions, turned a blind eye. She wasn't saying that this was going to explode and cripple the economy or anything like that, just that the world was ignoring an issue that would be impossible to ignore in the near future. It's amazing what people will believe when it's packaged up nice and shiny, and when they think everyone else thinks the same thing: somebody has to be looking out for us, right?

Well, bad news my friends, nobody is looking out for us and we are being played. This whole commercialized THC thing isn't going to end well.

I'm going on record saying this so that when the finger-pointing starts in a few years, I can rest easier knowing at least I threw it out there. I saw some data that the state released in its first report[12] mandated by the Colorado House of Representatives in 2016. Between the painfully whitewashed veneer and attempts at putting the best foot forward was some straight scary stuff—and nobody seems to be paying attention.

That same week, I had a day in treatment where the only two people who checked in were there for weed, just plain old weed. One of them described the psychosis he felt in detail when he smoked without knowing there was a word for what he was describing.

I also spoke with a brilliant chemist who walked my wife and me through the science and explained, over the course of hours, how all of the estimates of potency in weed in Colorado are low, and that we are just starting to realize how behind The Industry we are. For those of you unfamiliar with the potency issue when I got sober in 1996 weed was about 4 percent THC (that's the part of the plant that gets you high). Today the national average is above 12 percent and Colorado is seeing THC in plant concentrations of over 40 percent and concentrates that top 95 percent THC.

Additionally, a huge study[13] was released showing that people

---

12 Marijuana Legalization in Colorado: Early Findings, March 2016, produced by the Colorado Department of Public Safety

13 *American Journal of Psychiatry*, April 22, 2016, "Cannabis, Psychosis and Mortality: A Cohort Study of 50,373 Swedish Men."

who started smoking weed in adolescence had decidedly shorter lives than those who hadn't. This, in addition to the well-established link between early frequent use and psychosis.[14]

Then, a group of Southern Colorado hospitals came out publicly in opposition to retail THC shops in their community of Pueblo. The Colorado Springs newspaper *The Gazette* reported that at one hospital, "nearly half of the newborns born last month at their facility who were drug tested due to suspected pre-natal exposure tested positive for marijuana."

Colorado now has the highest marijuana use rates in the nation, with 33 percent of users reported using THC daily. While overall arrests for marijuana were down statewide, people under eighteen made up almost half of all those arrested for THC in 2014, almost double from 2012. And while fewer white kids were arrested for weed, many more minority youths were: 29 percent Hispanic and 58 percent black youths.

Mandated treatment for driving under the influence increased 48 percent for weed as the primary drug listed since its commercialization.

Meanwhile, it was 4/20, the official weed holiday in Colorado, and everywhere I turned people were making jokes about it, lighting up, and the advertisements were everywhere; they were relentless. Every celebrity stoner on earth came to Denver for a concert, show, or whatever and several of them got so wasted they couldn't perform. It happens all the time but this felt bigger since so many were affected and I was considering all of the above-mentioned facts.

Here is what I think will occur. The data will show a worsening situation but fewer people in power will pay attention to it. Even if

---

14 *The Lancet*, volume 5, no 5, pages 380-81, Published May 2015.

lawmakers do eventually wake up to what is really happening, by this time The THC Industry will be dug in like a tick and we will have a hell of a time reining them in. Their hefty political donations will continue to immobilize lawmakers. By the time we've reached a point where lawmakers have to act, such a large portion of the population in Colorado will be consuming THC that it would be like trying to bring a "don't drink wine" message to France.

As perceived risk continues to drop due to advertising campaigns by The Industry, youth use will continue to increase. As weed gets even stronger and concentrates play a larger role in our culture, mental health will suffer in ways that will be obvious to those of us in the field but tough to measure. With nobody challenging The Industry spin machine, their messaging will be all that people hear. It will take original and critical thought to see through that spin, but right now I see little to none of that now.

Traffic safety won't get any better because impaired drivers will continue to do their thing at higher levels, and prosecuting them will get harder because of current cases as well as the erosion of the 5ng/ml threshold, so fewer will be arrested. Those who are arrested will be able to mount more successful defenses as case law grows.

As the next generation grows up in a place where pervasive THC use is accepted and even encouraged, we will see the harmful effects of weed on the brain and body play out much faster because they will be using stronger stuff more often at earlier ages.

Politicians will bury their heads in the sand when public health and law enforcement talks and hold their hands outstretched when The Industry lobbyists walk into the room. Laws will change slowly no matter how much the population yells because money drives this country, not public health or concern for our future, unless of course that future is next quarter's returns.

This isn't going to end well, for us in Colorado at least. Many of you call Colorado the "experiment." I think the "sacrificial lamb" might be more accurate. Pay attention so that the problems manifested here from this failed experiment are not repeated more often than necessary. Learn from the mistakes made, and let the damage done in my home state be a warning to yours. The grass isn't greener on this side.

Resources

There Is an "A" for Everything

AA (Alcoholics Anonymous)*

International, nonprofessional mutual-aid fellowship for alcoholics, to help them "stay sober and help other alcoholics achieve sobriety." Famous for the Twelve Steps, a program of spiritual and character development. No age requirement, no fees, and open to all people who suffer from alcoholism.

NA (Narcotics Anonymous)*

Nonprofit fellowship for people who are recovering drug addicts who meet together to help each other stay clean. A program of complete abstinence from all drugs. No religious, political associations. Program called the Twelve Steps and Twelve Traditions of NA. Primary service is the NA group meeting.

MA (Marijuana Anonymous)*

Similar to AA and NA, but for people addicted to marijuana. Adopts the AA Twelve-Step program.

CA (Cocaine Anonymous)*

Same as AA, MA, NA, but for people addicted to cocaine. They also accept people who are recovering addicts of alcohol and mind-altering substances. Also utilizes AA's Twelve Steps.

CMA (Crystal Meth Anonymous)*

Similar to previously mentioned support groups. Although they also adopt the AA Twelve Steps, they insist that their Twelve Steps are unique because of the specific darkness, compulsions, and paranoia associated with meth use, as well as the hyper-intensity and long-term use.

OA (Overeaters Anonymous)

Similar, but for people who suffer from compulsive overeating. Employs Twelve Steps and traditions.

LGBTQ Twelve Steps

Twelve-Step programs for people in the LGBTQ community suffering and recovering from any substance addiction or addictive behaviors.

All of these programs are anonymous and focus on addicts helping each other. Their only requirement is that members must have a desire to recover from their addictions and publicly have been given permission from AA to configure their Twelve-Step program to suit each group's mission.

Those things are free! They pass a collection basket to pay to rent the facility they use for the meetings. People usually donate a dollar, but you don't need to do that if you're just checking it out. Enjoy the semi-climate-controlled church basement and awful coffee, there's no charge man! If you need professional help you need to do some

research. Addiction is a disease and should be treated by professionals, not people who are just selling stuff. Investigate and ask lots
of questions. Ask people who have been there themselves; they will
have ideas.

Once you have discerned that you have a good person and/or
team in place to help, you will need to trust them, sometimes with
some really big stuff that can be hard to deal with. With that in
mind, make sure that you are working with decent people who are
there to truly help you and other addicts, and not just trying to cash
in on your desperation; there is plenty of that nonsense out there.
**Bottom line: keep asking, keep working, and don't give up—there
is always hope!**

Glossary

Let's Talk Weed

It is very interesting to me how we have evolved in our use of language around THC in the last few years. One of the most obvious examples involves the word "prohibition." For years, the word was only used when talking about the prohibition of alcohol in the 1920s and early 1930s. But the word came back into fashion with the 2012 campaign. The use was slick because it got people to associate marijuana use with alcohol use, one of the main goals of the campaign. Prohibition is a word with negative connotations in the minds of most Americans. It makes us think of sour-faced teetotalers, flappers and speakeasies, and violent mobsters like Al Capone shooting up Chicago, more than simply forbidding the sale of alcohol. By talking about the "prohibition of cannabis" we sound super official, don't we! Sounds a heck of a lot better than saying the "commercialization of weed."

Newsweek magazine's special edition on weed (entitled *Weed 2016*) was more like a love song to marijuana. The cover read, "Is this the end of pot prohibition in America?" When the cover of *Newsweek* uses "prohibition" the marketing propaganda has hit mainstream.

Another notable change is the use of the word "cannabis." Using the scientific name for the plant sounds so high end, so legitimate. It sounds way better than "pot" or "weed." When people who aren't scientists or medical professionals use the word "cannabis" around me I can make some pretty sound assumptions about where they stand on this issue.

Another word I'm hearing more and more is "medicate." One of my favorite guys on YouTube goes by "customgrow420." He has nearly 800,000 followers and dozens of videos. Since he isn't in a state where recreational THC is illegal he calls getting high "medicating." I love it! I watched a video where this dude ate 200-plus milligrams of THC candy and said he was feeling "really medicated." Note to the reader: medicated = wasted, at least for "customgrow420."

Here is a list of "official" definitions:

✓ **420**

> Lots of rumors about the origins, I don't really care about that stuff. Today it means getting high. For instance: "420-friendly" is a somewhat stealth way of saying the place is weed-friendly. April 20—4/20— is the stoner holiday.

✓ **710**

> Hopefully you didn't skip the chapter dedicated to this. In case you did read it and just forgot in the flood of information, 710 is "OIL" upside down and is the number associated with smoking concentrates. July 10—7/10—is the holiday.

✓ **3750**

> Weed and crack smoked together.

✓ A-Bomb

Marijuana smoked with heroin.

✓ Baked/Blazed/Blunted/Blitzed/Couch-Locked

These are all creative ways of saying someone is high on THC. Being "high" is a bit passé; most users would refer to themselves a bit more creatively.

✓ Black Market

The non-taxed "illicit" sale of marijuana. Much attention is given to the expanding/contracting Black Markets in states with legalized/commercialized THC as both a justification for and case against.

✓ Blaze

Smoke weed.

✓ Blunt

A cigar with the tobacco leaves removed and then refilled with weed. The good ones are sealed with honey and rolled from Phillies or White Owl cigars. Being "blunted" is another way of expressing intoxication via THC. It becomes a "B-40" if you dip it in malt liquor (St. Ides was always my favorite) then let it dry before smoking it. It becomes a "candy blunt" when you dip it in cough syrup. As you can imagine, those doing this get wasted-er.

✓ Bong

This is like a big tube with water in that you pull smoke through. Pretty tough to picture if you haven't seen one so just Google it. Basically a tool for smoking that takes up a ton of space and frequently spills nasty-smelling water if you are careless/really stoned.

✓ Bowl

A smoking apparatus that looks like a pipe. Also another way of measuring when you are hard up: "Don't know man, only have about a bowl left and I need that for the morning."

✓ Bud

The buds of the weed plant. People like to smoke this very potent part of the plant to get high.

✓ Budtender

Someone who works in a dispensary. In many cases holding this job gives them a platform to dispense medical advice and for some reason people listen. Budtenders are people who have smoked a bunch of weed and are now living the dream because they get to stand behind a counter and earn $12 per hour selling it; typically not doctors.

✓ Chronic

If you're my age it might mean a pretty dope album that Dre dropped back when he was a rapper. It can also mean weed, usually pretty strong weed.

✓ Dabbing

Smoking concentrates. Bad and stupid, don't do it. Read that chapter!

✓ Dank

Traditionally, this was a way of describing really strong weed (see Chronic) but today it is a way of describing all things good. Example: "that party was fully dank" "my new car is dank" "last night was dank." Use this word sparingly old people or you run the risk of sounding like a total dork. I have attempted to incorporate this word into talks with teenagers only to leave them laughing at me and realizing that I am probably much older than I look and way nerdier than I perceive myself.

✓ Denver Broncos

Best football team in the NFL 1997/1998/2015. Fact. Second best team in the NFL '77, '86, '87, '89, '13.

✓ Dispensary

A state-sanctioned store that sells marijuana and THC-based products.

✓ Ditch Weed

Weak weed. Used to mean under 3 percent THC. Today, ditch in Colorado is anything 15 percent or under.

✓ Doobie

Term for a big ol' joint back in the day. Think of the Rock and Roll Hall of Fame band the Doobie Brothers—yes they smoked a lot and were brothers in weed, definitely better than their original name, Pud— and you will get a handle on the timeframe. If you still call it a doobie, you are really dating yourself.

✓ Flower

This is weed in the form that most of us recognize; a plant. When someone says "flower" they mean weed in plant form.

✓ Forms of Measurement

Weed is sold by weight, for the most part, these are the typical measurements and their slang:

Nickle: $5 worth of weed, enough to get high once.

Dime: $10 worth of weed, this should get you and a friend good and blunted.

Dub/20 Sac: A little less than an eighth of an ounce of weed. I had a buddy in high school who had a vanity license plate that read "dubsac" he got pulled over a bunch. When you buy most drugs in open-air markets (typically pretty scary places) this is the standard measurement. When asked "how many" by the dealer, the number you respond with signifies the number of 20 bags you want to buy.

Eight: ⅛th of an ounce, a pretty typical measurement for sales.

Quarter: ¼th of an ounce.

Ounce/Z: You guessed it, an ounce of weed or THC product. This is a pretty solid amount of weed/THC. Back in the day it would get me and the gang good and high for a weekend, today it is the legal limit that a non-state resident can buy at once, and half what a Colorado resident can buy in one stop per day. Since this limit applies to concentrates in Colorado as well, one can easily buy a month's worth of concentrate at each stop, each day, as a non-resident.

QP: A quarter-pound of weed.

Pound: Lots and lots of weed, way more than someone would ever need for personal consumption.

✓ **Gray Market**

Typically, this refers to diverted marijuana from dispensaries being sold into the Black Market. It is often grown "legally" but sold in an illegal market.

✓ **Greenout**

We are all pretty familiar with the term "blackout" associated with drinking. A "greenout" is when you have the same experience with weed. This describes being so intoxicated on THC that one can't remember the events that took place while high. Search YouTube for lots of examples of users in greenouts and for a "greenout survival guide" posted by "Lex Blazer." Mr. Blazer assures us that greenouts are not dangerous and that we should drink water, sipping it slowly, and that we often feel better after throwing up so "keep a bucket handy." I would like to point out that being in a state in which one cannot remember what took place has the potential to be pretty dangerous depending on what is going on around that person. I also wonder about the rationale behind issuing a survival guide for something that's hallmark is the inability to remember anything? There must be something to the guide, however; it does have 22k views.

✓ **Indica**

A species of the cannabis genus that is considered to be more relaxing/sedating than its cousin Sativa.

✓ **Joint**

The dried plant rolled in paper and smoked like a cigarette.

✓ **Kind/Keif/Kush**

All used to refer to specific types of weed but are now used generically to describe marijuana.

✓ **Medical Marijuana**

Marijuana and marijuana-derived products with the word "medical" written before them.

✓ **Medicating**

Another way of saying getting high on THC. Watch some YouTube, "I'm so medicated right now bro."

✓ Reefer

Another term for marijuana. From the Spanish *grifa*, a 1930's Mexican slang term for a pot-smoker. It was popularized by the 1936 film *Reefer Madness*, a cult classic about drug dealers who turn teens into addicts by introducing them to reefers, wild parties, and jazz. Nobody says "reefer" anymore—unless you are The Lobby and yell "Reefer madness!" anytime anyone says anything about THC that you don't like.

✓ Sativa

A species of the cannabis genus that is considered to be more invigorating than its cousin Indica.

✓ Shake

What's left over after trimming the bud. Used to roll joints and blunts but most importantly to make concentrates.

✓ Terpene

Fragrant oils that make weed smell "good." They are not at all confined to cannabis, but are most often discussed by weed aficionados who like to compare them to the bouquet people discuss with fine wine. If someone is talking terpene, they are either trying really hard to sound cool or super-experienced weed smokers.

✓ Top Shelf

Strong weed. Just like top-shelf booze at bars, now it is actually on the top shelf at stores, the figurative becomes literal in Colorado.

About the Author

Illustration by Landon Cort

In 2007, Ben Cort left his role as a director at a Denver-based S&P 500 firm to help start a nonprofit called Phoenix Multisport. This career move was the first time that Ben joined his vocational life and his recovery; he has been a part of the field since.

Over the last ten years, Ben has been a leader inside of several Colorado-based nonprofits, including the substance abuse treatment program at The University of Colorado Hospital. His work on various boards, in the media, and within his community has allowed Ben ample opportunity to do what he loves most—help point those suffering from addiction towards recovery.

Ben's own recovery from addiction fuels all that he does professionally, including the founding of an organization called Addiction Treatment Marketers Organization (ATMO) that works to establish ethical standards for marketing and admissions professionals inside of the treatment field.

Between his ethics trainings and marijuana-related education, Ben speaks live to tens of thousands of people each year all across the country, including mental health professionals, kids and educators, law enforcement, medical professionals, corporate leaders, professional athletes, government officials, and parents.

Ben consults within the treatment field, as well as with state governments, the National Football League (NFL) and the National Football League Players Association (NFLPA).

When he isn't working, Ben loves nothing more than spending time with his wife and kids (in that order). Anything that involves a fly rod, tent, motorcycle, or good book is sure to distract him in his spare time.

For more information, contact Ben at *www.cortconsult.com*.